SUBPRIME FELON

INSIDE FEDERAL PRISON CAMP

PYERSE DANDRIDGE

ISBN 978-0-692-60938-5

Author photo by Nichelle Broadway, Broadway Forever
Photography, www.broadwayforeverphotography.com

Front cover design by Tatiana Vila, www.viladesign.net

Interior design by Williams Writing, Editing & Design,
www.williamswriting.com

With gratitude and appreciation,
I dedicate this book to my parents,
Mr. Tracy and Sonya Smith.
You two are the reason this memoir was possible.

Contents

Introduction

I don't consider myself an expert on anything prison-related. My purpose is to share my experience with the hope of educating those who are unaware of this lifestyle and world. Maybe I can ease the mind of a family member who has a son or husband going to Herlong Camp. Or maybe I can spark a conversation that possibly solves problems in our community. Perhaps someone in the same situation can be inspired by understanding my approach to prison camp and turn their experience into a positive one.

This book will focus on how I dealt with and handled the prison camp culture and environment. It's not a hard, flashy tale about how prison toughened me into a hardened brother. It is an exploration of my thoughts and feelings on the experience and why I believe it was the best experience that I ever had. One of my mottos in camp was "Why think about prison camp as a bad thing if I don't want anything bad to happen?" Out of respect for the individuals' privacy, I've changed the names of COs, inmates, and anyone else involved.

It was an experience that put my life in front of me and made me look at everything that I did, both right and wrong, with fresh eyes. My year at Herlong was an experience that made me appreciate every life much more than I ever had. That experience was a lesson in both tolerance and patience. It was also a lesson in gratitude and appreciation, and it was my best chance to get the career I want started.

I never want to go through it again. However, I would never replace the experience for the life of me.

Day One

On May 12, 2011, I started the day at four in the morning by saying good-bye to my stepdad, who was just waking up to wish me luck. From there, my mom dropped me off at Pierce Sr.'s house just before she went to work. I hugged her good-bye. It was the first time we'd hugged in years. We're not a real affectionate family. However, anyone could tell how much we loved each other. The fact she hugged me meant that she knew that I was going on a crazy journey. She couldn't do anything but watch on the sidelines like a stressed-out, emotional quarterback watching his defense hold the other team.

Pierce was still sleeping when I got to his house. I entered without waking him and lay down on his couch. I actually managed to sleep until he woke me. We talked for a few minutes. I could tell that he was nervous about that drive. The two of us had a lot of issues in the past. It was one of the reasons that I call him Pierce and not Dad, and why I prefer my name to be spelled Pyerse instead of Pierce. However, that day, I saw in his eyes that he was going to take his son to prison. We both knew that I was going to a camp, which wouldn't be like the prisons on television. However, at that moment I felt like he was doing the saddest task that he ever had to do. He wanted to do it because he knew how hard it would be for me to get there on my own. And maybe he just wanted to say a few last words to me and see me one last time. Whatever his reasons were, I know they were probably the most genuine I've ever felt from him.

After he took a shot of brandy, we started the drive to Herlong. He gave me $40 and told me not to pay him back. He just wanted to make sure that I had some money on my books at the camp. I had another $30 with me.

We left at about eight in the morning. The drive was full of Top 40 music and light conversation. We pulled over near Applegate to get some breakfast at a mom-and-pop diner.

However, when we got to Reno, that's when I started to feel like "Damn, I'm really on my way to prison."

I could tell by his vibe that Pierce felt the same way. My whole case was still annoying him. I was a college graduate and a struggling writer working as a busboy at a local restaurant. I was convicted of one count of bank fraud because I helped with an equity-skimming mortgage fraud. I bought five homes with the help of a loan officer who helped alter tax documents and bank statements and loan documents to help me get homes. In return he, his broker, and the real estate agents would collect their respective commissions for every house. The five houses I got were worth less than the mortgage I paid. To help pay for these homes, an appraiser adjusted the value of the homes to the highest value. From there, the real estate agents, loan officer, and escrow agent adjusted their commissions to give me a cash advance. A few times, the loan officer created false paperwork which stated that the home needed work and a contractor would get the excess money. Instead, that money come to me.

To my knowledge, only the loan officer went to prison camp, about three years after I returned from the halfway house. He got the same seventeen-month sentence I received, according to the Federal Bureau of Prisons website. I have no idea whether the broker or any of the agents received any punishment.

Pierce felt, as did many of my friends and family, that I was manipulated by the broker and loan officer. The prosecution and my public defender felt that I was young and didn't know any better. In fact, my public defender told me that the government didn't want me in prison. However, due to the guidelines, it was their job to put me there. My family believed that I shouldn't have gone because many people have fake records and screwed the banks for years with real estate. Rightly or wrongly, those were the thoughts that were going through Pierce's head.

I just took it in stride. I didn't like the idea of going to prison. In fact, it was very depressing to know that I was going. However, I just told myself, "If God put it on my to-do list, it must be because I can handle it." That quote didn't make the drive any less daunting.

We arrived at Federal Corrections Institute, Herlong, a medium-security institution, at about noon. I gave Pierce my jacket, hugged him for the first time in years, and then went into the building.

I walked into the lobby and said, "Hello, I'm a self-surrender," to the correctional officer, or CO, at the front desk and metal detector. He was Latino and the same height as me, and he wore a white officer's shirt with a black tie. He had a nametag and a cap. He always had a smirk on his face. I later wondered if he took me seriously. Clearly, that situation meant more to me than to him. I was numb and void of emotion; I wasn't sad or happy. I was just trying to brace myself for whatever could happen.

After putting my wallet on the conveyor belt, I walked through the metal detector. When I reached to get my wallet, the CO stopped me and took my wallet. I didn't do or say anything as he went through my wallet, asking me if I had any weapons or drugs. I told him no.

When he pulled out my money, I asked, "That goes on my books, right?"

He smirked. "Yeah, it goes on your books." Not that I could do anything if he pocketed it.

He made me sign a document that stated that I had $70 as well as some liability stuff that I didn't understand.

He took me to a cell that was about the size of my bathroom at home. It had a metal toilet and brick walls painted white. The floor was concrete. There was a bench near the wall. From that bench, I could look out the window at the COs working at a long desk and an inmate, with a pressed, tan collared shirt tucked in his pants and a fabric belt, sweeping the floors. At the time, I assumed that I'd be wearing that same outfit.

There was also a large metal door in the far wall which looked heavy. I later learned that I was in the processing and receiving area. This is where they get the inmates ready to come and go from the FCI. This was the first time I heard the COs' keys slapping their thighs as they walked back and forth, which annoyed and scared me throughout the time I was at camp.

While I was waiting, I started to lose track of time and my sense of time as well.

Later, the same CO walked me to a room and asked me what was my size. I told him a 34 waist and a large in shirts. He then said, "If there are any drugs on you, you'll get put into the hole and hit with another charge."

Then he told me to strip down. I stripped down to my underwear and socks. He said, "No, strip down." So I took everything off. As he put gloves on, he told me to turn around and bend over and open my cheeks. I did as told without question. Looking back, it was obviously humiliating, but my mind was blank at the time.

The CO did nothing. He didn't even move. The experience took less than five seconds. I don't know if he was trying to scare me, look at my butt, or get a kick out of it. Maybe he was just trying to do his job to the bare minimum. I turned back around and he gave me some blue slip-on shoes, white socks, boxers, white T-shirt, and a green jumpsuit. He then put me into another holding cell.

I sat on the floor, folded my legs and after a good stretch meditated. At home I practiced meditation and yoga with YouTube videos. Since I was probably going to wait for a long while, I figured I might as well meditate and do some yoga. I was trying to keep my mind focused. I didn't want to sit in that cell and stare at the wall. I figured meditation was a good way to pass the time.

The CO looked through the window and said, "You can sit on the bench."

I could tell he was trying not to laugh at me. I just cheerfully told him that I was fine. I still had some good nature in me. I kept thinking about how being in prison was going to better my career. I had it set in my mind that I would reflect on what I'd done wrong and come back stronger than ever before. It was my chance to hit the reset button and launch my life in a positive direction.

Next I was escorted to another room, a few feet from the holding cell, where a nurse asked me some basic health questions about my smoking habits, sexual activities outside of prison, and if I had any diseases or injuries. After that, I was quickly escorted back to my cell. Minutes later, I was taken to another building where they gave me my prison ID card and bedding. As we went through each door, the CO escorting me had to wait for someone to buzz him in.

Several of the doors in this area had had to be opened by someone at a control panel. I later found out this was the processing and receiving building where COs recorded incoming and outgoing inmates from both the camp and the FCI. The CO would radio another CO or lieutenant to ask them to open the door to take me to the next room. The doors that didn't need to permission for us to enter, the CO used any one of several keys on his hip. I was still numb as I patiently waited for the officer to do his job.

When we stepped outside, my eyes was immediately attracted to the fences reaching the clouds. There was nothing outside but concrete, metal, and dirt as we passed between the buildings. We went to another building, which turned out to be the main processing building I went to when I self-surrendered. Once inside, it felt like another world. Though the room had proper lighting, it seemed dark and disconnected from everything that I knew. By this time, I was totally twisted around. Throughout each room, the CO was never more than an arm's reach away from me.

He told me, "Okay, you can stay in another holding cell for two days because we don't have any vans to take you to the camp, or you can walk to the camp."

I wasn't sure when he found out about this, but I just wanted to get out of there.

"Are there any landmines out there?" I asked, holding my bedding.

"Naw, but there are a few coyotes." He smirked. "But you'll be fine." He told me to follow the road around and I'd see the camp.

It was about a mile walk through the parking lot and down the empty two-lane road that connected the FCI to the camp. I walked on the road until a car zoomed past me at about 60 mph. I then walked on the rocky dirt parallel to the road. There was nothing but dirt and sage plants on either side of the road. On one side of the road there was a large wall about twenty feet long and

9

ten feet high parallel to the road. To this day, I have no idea what that wall was for or how it got there. About halfway though my walk I could see the camp. It had two buildings: the camp dorms to my left, and the administrative and food service building to my right. Inmates sitting outside the administrative building pointed to the left as if I was to walk in there. I later found out that inmates not only knew when the camp was getting new inmates, but they could tell I was new and confused because I had bedding in my hands.

I walked through the camp dormitory's double doors and went to the CO's office. A few feet from the double doors were two television sets about four feet apart. The CO's office was between the two televisions. These were the Whites' and Asians' television sets, though anyone could watch with them if they chose to. After work there was always five to fifteen inmates sitting there watching them. The TVs were in a major walkway, so these inmates would sit against the backs of the bunk beds to allow inmates and officers to walk around them. That was normal at that time of the day. I don't remember seeing any inmates inside when I first arrived. However, there were tons of inmates at the door. In fact, they stared at me the whole time I was there, so they told me.

The CO inside the office was a tall, dark-haired, White man in a blue uniform. He assigned me to my bed on the freeway.

The freeway was a high-traffic area which had bunks along the walkway. He gave me my mattress and assigned me to the bottom bunk. Underneath the bunk were two empty boxes and an empty slot. The thin mattress sat on top of a hard metal frame. The bed was about six feet long but barely three feet wide, which was the same for all the beds at this camp.

Minutes later, a few Black inmates walked up to me and gave me hygiene (deodorant, soap, toothbrushes, etc.) and snacks. I was afraid to take them at first because I was afraid of getting taken advantage of, like in some old prison stories I heard. However, they told me it was cool, and I figured what the hell. Inmates had to provide their own hygiene items, and current inmates would help the incoming inmate get situated until they could go to the commissary. Sometimes inmates arrived between commissary days, and they sometimes didn't have money for several weeks because they didn't have money saved or a job.

I told a few brothers that I was from Sacramento, and the next thing I know a brother from there walked up to my bunk and talked to me. I tried to explain my crime to him, but I'm not sure whether I explained it correctly or he just didn't get it. He soon got bored with me and left.

They also gave me advice, such as to refer to all the male COs only by their last names. All female COs were referred to as Ms. and their last or first name, whichever the CO preferred. A lot of inmates' advice didn't have a reason; it was as if I had to do it because they said so. I found out we addressed the COs in that manner because we were not free like them. That was one of the ways we gave them respect.

After that, I changed into some shorts, which one of the brothers gave me. I took a tour with a brother I'll call Brother Cooker, who taught Bible lessons at the camp.

Federal Prison Camp, Herlong is a satellite prison camp, which means it's a camp within, or around, a larger institution. In this case, FPC Herlong is a satellite camp to FCI Herlong, which is a medium-security prison, or as we called it, the medium. There was not a low-security or other prison in the area. There were rumors of the Feds building one, but I don't know it was true. The purpose of the satellite camp was to assist the medium and to help it function. The campers would do tasks that the inmates at the medium couldn't do because they were considered a security risk. We processed orders, received deliveries, and drove low-risk inmates to the hospital. We even did community service for the community of Herlong, California.

The camp was built on an old Army base. I heard that our dorm room was an actual Army barracks that were modified for prison security. The other rumor I heard was that contractors completed the plumbing and major electric of the dorm room and inmates did the furniture and doors.

It was one massive room, with bunks and lockers for all the camp inmates. There were 136 inmates living in this room, sometimes less because inmates would transfer to other prisons or go home. The dorm was full of inmates who self-surrendered and inmates who transferred, or worked their way down, as those inmates put it, from other institutions. Those inmates who transferred usually came from higher-security institutions all over the United States, such as United States Penitentiary, Lompoc (a high-security prison), FCI Victorville Medium II (a medium-security prison), and FCI Safford (a low-security prison).

All of the inmates at camp were nonviolent. To qualify for camp (or have camp status), an inmate couldn't have any sexual or violent crimes. Also, there is a point system. If an inmate had less than twelve points, he could have camp status. I went into camp with one point.

To my knowledge, inmates at the low-security prisons have at least twelve points. Inmates at the medium- and high-security prisons would have considerably more than twelve points. The inmates who transfer here are transitioning into a halfway house to help readjust to civilian life. However, inmates who self-surrender, such as myself, are sentenced to camp because that was the fairest punishment. If the government sent someone like me to a low-security prison, that punishment could be deemed harsh according to the sentencing guidelines that most federal judges follow.

The dorm room was divided by the walkways and freeway into different living sections. Each section had four living quarters, each having two lockers, a twin-size bunk bed, and a desk.

Surrounding the living section were the four televisions that were mounted at the highest point of the walls. In addition to those televisions, there was three smaller rooms, each with a television. The televisions were controlled by inmates, usually the one who was in the room first.

The laundry room had six washers and six dryers, an

ice machine, tables to fold laundry, ironing boards, and a hot water dispenser.

Next to the CO's office was a computer room where inmates could check their emails via TRULINCS, the Trust Fund Limited Inmate Communication System. This system was where we got email from our loved ones and it was where we accessed memos from the warden and other administrators. The system was very limited when I was there. Even the copy and paste functions were removed. It was very basic, even more basic than the Notepad application on most computers.

Our loved ones would have to send emails from a site called CorrLinks. Once the email was complete, the inmate might have to wait two hours to receive it because the email was scanned for fraud or other possible violations. Once a message was received, inmates could respond to our loved ones, who had the same waiting period. It cost me five cents a minute to access the emails, regardless whether I sent an email or not. To access the memos from the warden or other administrators was free. It was also free for my loved ones to access the emails via CorrLinks on their desktop.

The law library, next to the computer room, had up-to-date files on court cases and past cases and laws. I've seen more people in that library than the other library, and some of them came out damn near lawyers.

Outside the barracks were the barber shop, leisure library, cafeteria, commissary, and administration buildings. In the administration building, there was a very small exercise room with old treadmills and exercise machines. However, the monitors and most of the wires were removed from the machines. I understood it was for security reasons, but some inmates told me the wires were stolen by other inmates. There were also rooms for hobbies and crafts, with lockers for inmates with permission. Finally, there was a multipurpose room that was used for working out and church services. The medical services were also in this building, and those rooms stayed locked until the nurses arrived.

Inmates could play sports on three full-size basketball courts and a handball court with a wall made by inmates from the camp maintenance department, called GM6 or General Maintenance Six. A baseball diamond was just a few feet away from the courts. Next to the baseball diamond was a soccer field that was outlined with black asphalt for running, which we called the small track. About four laps around this track was a mile. If we wanted a longer run, we had a path that circled the soccer field, basketball courts, and the baseball diamond. Two laps around that path would be about a mile. Also, inmates had two gardens where we planted fruits and vegetables while the CO watched to make sure that no contrabands were hidden in the garden.

Near the mountains behind the camp were more buildings. Rumor had it that the military was building weapons there. Some people told me it was a decommissioned military base. Others told me that it was an alien base. Go figure. However, in the mornings we saw construction and delivery trucks going to and from those buildings. During the day, from the television room areas we also saw construction workers build and break down structures.

As far as the electrical parts from the treadmills, some inmates believed that they were stolen by inmates for whatever reason. The funny thing was that another inmate told me that the administration took them out because there was a federal law that banned wires in prison. I have never seen such a law, although I am not saying that it was not true. I learned on that first day that everyone lies here! God only knows what's true and what's not.

We were required to wear green collared shirts and green pants with black boots to work, to meet with an administrator, or anytime we were outside the dorm between 7 a.m. and 3 p.m. When we had visitors, we would also have to wear this uniform, which we called greens. Inside the dorm, we could wear sweats, T-shirts, or whatever we got from the commissary.

We were allowed to walk around the camp freely. There were no ten-minute moves (a ten-minute period when inmates were allowed to move about) and no gates. We were good as long as we stayed within the signs that said "out of bounds."

Later that day, one brother asked me if I needed anything else, and I said, "Yeah, a pen and paper.".

"Oh, just one piece of paper?"

"Naw, as much as you're willing to give me. I have a lot of writing to do." I then told him that I was thinking about starting a novel.

Suddenly, a CO screamed, "Count time!"

The inmates hustled to put chairs away and get back to their bunks. I would later find out that was the 4 p.m. count. Count time is when the COs count all the inmates in the camp and FCI to make sure no one escaped or was otherwise missing. There are two types of counts that are mostly used: regular count and bed book count.

Regular count was when the inmates stood in their squares as one CO walked up and down the aisles and counted the inmates, while the other CO stood in plain sight of the inmates to make sure no inmate moved. The camp CO and usually one CO from the FCI or food service would help with these counts. That was the count we had about 90 percent of the time.

The bed book count was when two COs walked together, one in front and one behind holding a book with pictures and ID numbers of all the camp inmates. When the COs walked up to an inmate, the first CO would check his ID. Each inmate had to state his last name and registration number. I would say, "Dandridge, 18523–097." The second CO would verify that number, and they moved on to the next bunk. The rule was that we had to remain standing until the COs were finished.

There was a third type of count, which was called the out count. Any time inmates were allowed to be outside of the dorms, whether in food service, a work assignment, or a community service project, the CO would do a simple roll call like a teacher would in grade school. That count didn't usually involve a second CO, though I've seen it happen in food service, and then it was reported to that CO's superior.

I was told to never miss a count time because it could be considered an escape and I would get disciplined. Count time was very important to all the COs. Their job was on the line if inmates were missing. Also, many COs felt that camp inmates get a lot of passes as for as how they are treated and they believed being in camp was a privilege and a reward, so the least a inmate could do was to stand still during count. Most counts only took five minutes, unless the COs were unorganized or mad at us.

My first dinner in camp was a blur to me. I stood quietly in the slow-moving line, surrounded by twenty or thirty inmates wearing their sweats and greens. I sat at a table with other inmates, but I didn't look at them. I stared at my food, but I didn't notice the food I was eating.

When I went back to my bunk, it hit me: "My ass is in prison." I knew it's a camp, but still, "Damn" was all I thought. At that moment, I felt as if I failed at life. It was going to be hard to make a good life after that. Everything I did previously was intended to help me to be a better Black man and a better member of society, and to improve my overall wellness. Instead, I committed a crime that put me in a prison camp and gave me a record, which all but nullified my bachelor's in English. All the work I did was for nothing, a complete waste of time. I started thinking that if I had been content with just bussing tables or living a middle-class life, then I wouldn't be there. There was also the feeling that no matter what I did from this point forward, it probably wouldn't matter because I'd fuck it up anyway and be right back at camp.

On top of that, I started to feel extremely lonely. I was used to being alone. In fact, I'd gone months without seeing a single friend. But this was real loneliness. It was like a disconnection from everything that I knew and loved and from the world altogether. Before coming to Herlong, when I was lonely at least I could call someone and go somewhere, or go to a movie by myself. That type of loneliness was depressing as hell. I remember being mad at myself for allowing opportunities to pass because I was working so hard at those restaurant jobs. I was mad at myself for doing something so stupid like getting those houses. I was mad at myself for not working harder to be the writer that I wanted to be.

Then I thought about how my degree was a waste. No way in hell I was going to make any use out of that. My diploma was going to be a poster on the wall at best. Maybe I could use it as a coaster or kindling. I would be working at dead-end jobs trying to pay off $72,000 in restitution.

For the first time in my life I felt like property. I was processed and received like property. I was put on that freeway like something people put to the side when they don't need it anymore. I couldn't come and go when I pleased. I couldn't talk to anyone unless I had permission. I could only do what I was allowed to do. I had seen campers with the words "Property of the US Government" on the back of their jackets, and assumed that I was going to wear that as well. The cavity check bugged me as well. I didn't even have the right to tell him no.

Just the thought that those COs could do anything they wanted however they wanted to do it made me feel like less than a nigger. I don't mean that as "dude" or "buddy" or "fellow Black person." I mean that as the lowest form of Black stereotype imaginable.

Luckily, every time I sank that low into depression, I snapped out of it. I reminded myself that my mom didn't raise any niggers. It was also the last time I used any form of "nigger" in my vocabulary. I respect those would want or need to use it. But for me, I'm not going to call anyone something I wouldn't want to call myself. People said it around me. I didn't like it, but I wasn't going to have that debate with them.

Then, I reminded myself that "what doesn't kill me makes me stronger." I thought about that concept that the "White man or devil is trying to send strong Black men to prison to keep us down." I'm not going to agree or disagree with that. Yet, at that moment, I was thinking "if the devil really was trying to stop me, he should have shot me in the head." God didn't put anything on my plate that I couldn't handle. I could clearly handle this prison camp thing. Instead of focusing on whether or not the White man or the devil was trying to stop me, I decided to find a way to make that camp an advantage, just like I told everyone that I would do.

I again thought about whether God or the devil put me here, especially which god, a Christian God or a cosmic being, or maybe a greater version of myself. At the time, I considered myself a Christian who was still struggling with the inconsistencies of the dogma. I returned to the church during my pretrial time because I felt it was a good way to look for something I didn't have an answer to. However, the more I questioned why I was there at Herlong, the more that I felt that if a Christian God put me there for punishment, it was unfair when bankers and businessmen have done the same crime I committed and they were not sentenced at all. Why on earth would He put me there? It seemed cruel to me and made me feel more abandoned.

How could I follow this Christian God whose divine will was to send me to a hellish place that could only benefit his archenemy? It felt like I was a good person thrown away because of a few mistakes. If I needed this type of punishment, couldn't there have been a way to do so without uprooting me and forcing me to start over? In addition, I've always felt freer when I wasn't trying to be Christian because then I didn't feel as if I was bounded by rules or dogma I didn't understand. It was at that moment that I decided I could no longer be a Christian.

All I wanted to do was go home. I thought I had enough of Sacramento. I didn't think I could go any further in that city because of everything I've been through. But when I was on that bunk, all I thought about was going home to Sacramento. Looking back, I think I just wanted to reconnect myself with my roots, my family, my social circle before I went anywhere else.

After a few deep breaths, I calmed down and I started writing my letter to my mom and worked on an outline for my novels.

That was my first day at prison camp.

My First Weeks

The camp was nothing like a war zone or zoo full of killers like I saw on television. In fact, the biggest problem with camp was that the inmates got bored fast. Luckily, I was so busy writing that boredom wasn't a problem, and I was reading more than ever. Even though I didn't like being there, I kept telling myself that I was blessed to sit in the library writing what would be this book while watching DVDs on a cheap TV/DVD combination. In between writing and watching DVDs, I would read as many books as I could.

The first few days, I stayed inside the dorm because I really didn't want to talk to people. I was very careful to stay away from anyone that would get me in trouble. I knew I had too much going on outside of the camp to be getting into trouble. I just wanted to keep to myself and only be around if needed for something. The dorm is where I did some of my best reading.

I hated being in my bunk for long periods of time. Because our living quarters were so small, it felt like we were crowding each other. With another inmate in the square there wasn't a lot of room to write. If I sat in the chair and used the desk, it would take up all the walking space in the square. Also, most of my bunkies would put their books or snacks on the desk, so there was no room. The only thing I could do is lie in bed, which wouldn't have made my stay productive. These squares were like our homes, though I refused to call it that because I wasn't going to be at camp long, and that place didn't feel like home to me.

As early as my second day at camp, I found out that most of the inmates kept their distance from me as well. Some inmates didn't know if I was a snitch. Others wanted to see how I dealt with prison and who I associated with. Some inmates greeted me quickly and wanted to be fast friends. I found those inmates to be the ones who were emotionally draining and needy for attention.

Beginning on my second day, I got out of bed at about seven in the morning. By the next week, I would be out of bed no later than six in the morning for breakfast. I pretty much stayed between the library, the tables in the dorm, or my bunk.

I also took the yoga classes offered at the camp. These classes were offered three days a week and taught by an inmate I'll call YT. A brief group meditation followed the classes. At home I had started regularly practicing yoga using YouTube videos. Because yoga was such a great stress reliever for me, it helped make my camp experience more manageable.

Before and after yoga class, I would spend my time in the leisure library. There I worked on my entrepreneurial ideas such as starting a news website or a production company. Next, I'd work on some novel and poetry ideas. It was during this time that I started experimenting using meditation music and sound. The R&B music I listened to at home wasn't available and the ton of religious music that was available I found distracting. However, there was also a ton of meditation music. Once I started experimenting with it, I was hooked.

By the end of the first seven days, I landed a job working for the powerhouse to learn HVAC and boilers. The powerhouse was where all the electricity for the prison and the camp was generated. I was recommended by an inmate named Frank. He wanted someone Black and intelligent to work with him because he wanted to have a better work environment.

About two weeks after arriving, I moved from the freeway bunk to my first and only bunk and locker. In cube number eight, I had the top bunk overlooking most of the televisions in the dorm from a distance. Some inmates called the group of four bunks their home, square, or cube. I called it my square or cube. I could hear the TV with my radio and headset just like at the drive-in movies. The locker had all my stuff in it, neatly, so I didn't have to cram everything into that box.

YT was be my first bunky. We were pretty much the same age, and we got along amazingly. He taught the yoga classes at the camp. We didn't talk too much in the bunks, mainly because I would be in the library, and he would be doing whatever he was doing. However, when we did talk it would always be comical because I would be silly, or we would talk about ideas for our post-prison life. We never interfered with our sleeping schedules, and we gave each other our privacy. We would alternate sweeping and wiping the square once a day.

During my first calendar month I had three meetings, one with the counselor to see if I had the mental stamina to handle prison camp, one with the case manager, and another one with the counselor for A&O (admission and orientation). I also had two meetings with the doctor and the dentist.

Football and basketball season made the time go by faster. In fact, that's usually when I'd watch television. A few times I'd watch a show like *NCIS: Los Angeles* or *The Young and the Restless*. But usually I'd watch the evening game or most of the big Raiders games.

Laundry at Herlong Camp

I did laundry two times a week. I might as well, it was free. There were six washers and six dryers that stayed full all day long. After I quit the powerhouse, I washed clothes twice a day. I only had one pair of sweat pants and four T-shirts plus two pairs of green prison uniform pants and three green prison uniform shirts, one long-sleeved and two short-sleeved, and underwear. I usually had a pair of green pants and a green shirt to wear while my clothes were washing. I showered twice daily: in the morning and when I came back from the library.

The washing machine used low-quality, watered-down liquid detergent that was administered by way of a button. I just needed to push the button to put the soap in the machine. However, the soap was so cheap, I would push the button several times to make sure I had enough soap to clean my clothes. If you were lucky you might get an inmate to put your clothes in the dryer for you and even fold them for free. Usually most inmates left your clothes on top of the dryer so they could use it.

I tried to wash my clothes in the early morning when people were sleeping or when everyone was at work.

Regardless of the size of the load, I, and most other inmates, used the hot water and heavily soiled settings. It was more water and electricity, but many inmates felt the prison wasted more resources than inmates could save through conservation.

Some inmates got skin irritation from the free soap and bought detergent from the commissary. Other inmates felt their clothes were cleaner after using the commissary detergent. I didn't want to spend any additional money at that place, and the free detergent cleaned my clothes just fine.

If my clothes needed repairs or got too small, I could replace them once a week on Friday. There was a laundry room next to the barbershop. I could get new prison green uniforms, underclothes, and travel-size hygiene items for free. Though hygiene items were available at the commissary, I took the free soap and deodorant to save money. This was the other reason I didn't want to pay money for detergent. If the green uniform got so dirty I needed to upgrade my detergent, I'd just wait until Friday morning and exchange it for a new one. I would have to purchase new sweats and underwear from the commissary, however.

Random Weather

I observed the weather from the big windows in the library. The weather for the most part was pretty mellow when I was there. However, I did see a mild snowstorm and a long period of rain. When the weather was really bad, we were not allowed outside. However the weather could suddenly worsen without warning. If the CO felt it wasn't safe for the inmates to be outside the dorm, he would have a yard recall, which forced all camp inmates to go inside the dorm.

There were times when it would rain for twenty minutes and then it was sunny all day long afterward. I remember seeing a bird in the air trying to go forward, but the wind was so strong that it drove the bird backward.

The winds would pick up without any warning. One time there was no breeze when suddenly a high gust of wind blew paperwork out of inmates' hands. The winds would push me backward hard when they were high. Sometimes you could hear the winds all night shaking and rattling the dorm.

In fact, I saw fifty-miles-an-hour winds cause a brownout. The winds were so strong that they pushed the dust inside the buildings and triggered the fire alarms. It was funny because the inmates didn't move. It was like they didn't trip off it. For twenty minutes, the alarms blared as inmates walked around making their theories and drawing their conclusions. However, I had never before heard of dust causing the alarms to sound. Other inmates mentioned that the vents were never cleaned; therefore there would be tons of dust and other things in the vents. After that the place smelled a whole lot dustier than ever before. When the alarm finally stopped, the place went back to normal. It was windy all night. I could hear the howling from inside.

The heating and cooling was pretty good, to be honest. While I was there, when the weather got too hot the AC would kick in as long as the doors stayed closed. The problem was that the inmates kept the front door open so the room barely cooled. It was the same with the library and the other rooms in the camp. The multi-purpose room had two doors, the main door and the emergency exit. The emergency exit wasn't allowed to be opened because it was a security risk. The camp admins thought that inmates would smuggle contraband into that room because it was so easy for a visitor to access it. However, if the inmates felt the room was too hot, they would open the emergency exit door and claim that the AC didn't work. We did that on weekends and nights.

Snow would fall in the winter. For the first few days, I loved it because instead of all the brown and gray, I saw white everywhere. However, after those few first days, the snow would look dirty and brown because the inmates traveled back and forth on it.

Temperatures at Herlong dropped to as low as 10 degrees when I was there. As long as I had my jacket and beanie, I actually enjoyed the weather. Luckily the dorm was warm enough so inmates wouldn't freeze, even though they still complained about the temperature. When I exercised outside, I wore thermals. However, at night I didn't always wear thermals because it was warm enough for me most nights. Other inmates wore them every night.

Summertime was hot, but it never got uncomfortable. The highs in the summer would be in the 90s and rarely hit 100 degrees.

Sleeping Conditions

I avoided being in my bed during the day. One reason was to avoid laziness. Another reason was to prevent inmates from talking to me when I didn't want to talk. I didn't mind talking, just not when I was trying to sleep or wanted some time to myself. I would usually find places where I could be alone for privacy.

The mattress I slept on wasn't very comfortable, but that was all that was available. As I mentioned before, the beds were about six foot long and three foot wide. Instead of a guardrail and a wall, there was a sheet of metal, about six feet high and six feet long, that connected the top and bottom bunks. It was high enough I could use the metal for back support when we watched television from the top bunks. The bunks were also bolted down. Our lockers and desk faced us and were one step in front of the beds. There was a ladder on my left side. Under that ladder I had my slippers, so I could immediately put them on to walk around. A shelf above the desk connected the two lockers. Attached to our lockers were the bunk beds for the neighboring inmates. About two feet from my bunky's locker, on the right, were the next inmates' quarters. I didn't have a neighbor behind me because the main walkway was behind me and to the left of me as well. I always found it funny that my bed from the freeway was directly behind me, because most inmates move quite a ways from their place on the freeway.

Also to my left was the window overlooking the food service building and courtyard. In the center of the courtyard was a massive light that shone through the windows onto my bed every night. The dorm lights were directly above me and shone right on top of me. After 10 p.m., the lights would be dimmed partially but still pretty bright. Because I couldn't sleep with blinders, I just got used to the sleeping situation. When I look back, I wonder how I tolerated it. However, if I am tired, I'll deal with just about anything to sleep.

Because the bed was so small, I slept on my side and shoulder, usually facing the lockers. At home, I would slept on my back or stomach. Because of the new sleeping position, I would sometimes wake up to shoulder and back stiffness. I would stretch out briefly then rush to breakfast after I made my bed. I was usually in my bed from 10 p.m. to 6 a.m. with an occasional nap.

One advantage to having the top bunk was I could watch TV from my bed. I was close enough to see the television, but far enough away to not hear other people while watching it. It provided a great sense of privacy. In addition, people didn't try to sit on your bed. Seeing inmates sitting on other inmates' beds left an uncomfortable feeling because it was hard to tell if that inmate kept himself clean or not. Some other inmates seeing it would even question both inmates' sexuality. If an inmate wanted to spend time at another inmate's square, they would stand or sit in the chairs.

During the night, inmates would cheer or laugh along with their favorite television shows while listening with their headphones, or converse at a low whisper or mumble, or play games. These inmates didn't have to work early in the morning because they either worked later or weren't required to work. However, once in a while the noise would disrespect those who had to be awake at six in the morning. Usually, a respected inmate of that individual's race would talk to the loud inmates. Doing so avoided conflicts and misunderstands.

However, those talking-tos didn't always stop the noise. For the inmates who slept closest to the televisions and television rooms, the noise was annoying. I slept on the opposite side of that area, so what I heard was like a whisper. Besides, I got into a routine and didn't have a problem getting to sleep.

In fact, right after the 10 p.m. count, I would fall asleep. I liked to get up in the morning and start my day. There was no need for me to lie in bed all day. Some inmates went to sleep at 8 p.m. and got up for the 10 p.m. count.

What bugged me was the COs' keys slapping their thighs when they did midnight, 2 a.m., or 5:30 a.m. counts. Usually, out of respect, COs would hold their keys so they didn't hit their thighs and wake up the inmates. Somehow I learned to sleep through that as well. Another thing that bugged me was that the COs would tap on inmates' beds to see if they were alive or in the bed. It happened to me once and I jumped out of my skin. The COs kept walking, and I fell back asleep.

Medical Care at FPC Herlong

The problem with medical at the camp was that the doctors were impersonal. My first doctor visit was a checkup to see if I was fit for prison. I was, but why did I get the exam in prison camp and not before? For some reason, I subconsciously thought the doctor was going to be a little nicer to me because we were both Black. Nope. She was cold and very strict about my card, which I forgot. She sarcastically told me, with zero eye contact, to go get my card, and she reminded me that I had to have it on me at all times. The whole exam took less than ten minutes. She checked the normal vital signs and reflexes. I asked a few questions and only got one- or two-word responses.

That same day I walked a few feet to the dentist's office. A dentist checked on my teeth. It was another impersonal doctor visit. He poked around in my teeth and mentioned that I had three missing wisdom teeth and another problem with my teeth that he didn't want to explain or clarify. He told me that my teeth were healthy and scheduled a cleaning for me. When I asked him why my teeth bled when I brushed, all he nicely said was that I could just need a cleaning and could be brushing wrong.

The room was small with two White dentists. One was middle-aged and balding, and the other was a chunky gray-haired man. I didn't get their names but I wouldn't have remembered anyway. It was a clean, cluttered room. I first sat on a plastic blue chair and then sat on a gray chair with a donut-shaped head rest. There were no chains, shackles, or restraints, and I was finished in five minutes. They scheduled me for a cleaning.

Two weeks later, I had a call-out to see the dentist. That visit would be my first visit to a dentist in years. It was supposed to be a cleaning, and they did that. However, when the dentist scraped all the plaque out from between my teeth, it felt like she was scraping the actual bone off the teeth. I felt that they were too rough with my gums. My mouth was killing me during the whole hour. I had a hard time keeping my mouth open the whole time. It was a helpless feeling. All I could do was sit there. I shook and squirmed a little, and stared at the light. Also, I was ordered to "open" and "lower my chin" and "turn left, turn right" while they physically made me comply. I hated every moment.

But it was free. I had one cavity and decay in one of my teeth. I guess they did a good job. I wanted to wait until I got home to get my teeth fixed. I didn't want to go through that again.

It was not worth losing work over. Hours afterward, my teeth would bleed when my tongue pushed against my teeth. Two hours later, my teeth still hurt. My bottom gums were sore. My decayed tooth was sore. The dental assistant, who was a camper, told me in the dorm that it was because I hadn't been to the dentist in years. However, other Blacks told me they had similar experiences.

About seven months into my sentence, I went to the doctor because I was having trouble breathing at night. I thought that was the reason why I was snoring at night. I hoped I didn't need anything, especially surgery, because I didn't want to be sick with a serious injury for months. It could take six months to get surgery if it was a non-emergency. One inmate with a hernia had been waiting for months for his surgery. I didn't want to knowingly be sick and have to wait for treatment. The doctor listened to my complaint and prescribed some nasal spray to loosen up my nostrils. That spray came three days later and did nothing for my snoring. Since my bunky said he wasn't bothered by my snoring, I stopped worrying about it.

About eight months into my sentence, I went to the doctor again because of my snoring and what I thought was asthma. My mom sent me some information that implied I might be allergic to the dry air or the sage plants. When I started running outside I noticed I had a hard time breathing. That was also around the time I noticed people complaining about my snoring—some jokingly, some seriously. When I finally got the call-out for the nurse, the nurse told me that she could give me an inhaler. However, I'd have to buy the allergy pills from the commissary. Unless I had no money on my books for six months, the nurses couldn't prescribe me anything if it was available at the commissary. Once I bought the allergy pills, I was breathing better but I still snored. That was more than I can say about the inhaler.

Ten months into my sentence, an inmate named Broadway got sick. For several days he walked around in a funk—zombie like—and didn't really talk or joke too much. Then he got so weak that he would have fallen over if someone didn't catch him.

People came to look at him in waves. The first wave was our nurse. The nurse looked at Broadway without touching him. He radioed his superiors at the FCI for permission to get the fire truck. Once the fire truck arrived, they contacted the paramedics. One of the paramedic ladies complained the inmates didn't have a lot of space in the cubes and went on to say that we looked like animals in there.

Soon employees from the Sierra Army Depot arrived and several men in suits who I didn't recognize. Before long, Broadway was rolled out, and the few who were watching gave him the thumbs up and he thanked us.

After a few people gossiped about it for a few hours, it was as if he wasn't there anymore. It was as if nothing happened.

These are the reasons I was afraid to get sick in prison camp. I knew they wouldn't let me die, if it was in their power to prevent it, but I just didn't want to feel like an animal. It was already bad enough I was property of the United States government. I didn't want my life depending on some emotionless CO or nurse going through bureaucracy and paperwork just so I could get necessary medical help.

Germs and Hygiene

One night around May 2011 a bunch of us Black inmates were in the sports TV room watching a NBA playoff game. I sat directly behind a brother eating a snack. Suddenly, I sneezed loudly in my elbow in what people called a vampire sneeze. An awkward silence followed.

One dude looked at me. When I asked, "What?" he just shook his head.

Suddenly, everyone was laughing at me.

Finally, someone who called himself T said to me: "We got a lot of germophobes in the place, man. We just don't like getting sick." That brother goes on to tell me to be sure that I cover my nose next time.

Another brother, who was sitting in front of me, Testimony, got nervous and changed his shirt.

Then the brothers in the room shared their stories about people and sneezing and getting sick.

I thought about that incident for most of the night. The health care there wasn't as good as I thought or was told. Why else would everyone be so afraid of being sick there?

The next morning I asked T, "Why don't they isolate the sick to keep germs from spreading?" I'd figure it would save the government money to only care for a minimum number of people.

"Yeah, they don't give a fuck, remember you are in prison. It ain't about money. Look at how much they spend on lights, shelter, food, bedding, laundry, water, hot water."

It's cheaper and more profitable to put a low-risk, low-danger criminal on an ankle bracelet than to pay for those things.

I understood why so many brothers asked if I had hygiene and made sure I had it. That was also why no one liked handshakes, why people touched objects with napkins, and why they took so many showers. If someone got sick, they could be out for two weeks. T told me to stay clean and keep up the hygiene. Good advice, because I didn't want to get sick there.

Everyone had to be clean, and some inmates cleaned their squares, or homes, daily. Some inmates washed clothes daily, like I did. I cleaned my cube every week because I was hardly in my square. I also took showers two to three times a day.

The only time I was sick with a flu, I was out of work for three days at the powerhouse. Frank and Testimony hooked me up with vitamin C pills, cough drops, and cough syrup. Other inmates would be sick for two weeks to a month. One inmate told me that while I was sick, ten other inmates were also sick. I believe that flu went around for about two months.

Food at Camp

We had a national, standardized menu of breakfast, lunch, and dinner from the Department of Justice that had a five-week rotation. The best meal was lunch because of burger Wednesdays and chicken fryer legs on Tuesdays and Thursdays. Dinner meals ranged from pastas to pork chops. Food service workers and inmates who were assigned to work during any lunch and the dinner shift throughout the week were allowed to eat at 6:00 a.m., 9:30 a.m., and 3:30 p.m. All other camp inmates were served at 6:00 a.m., 10:30 a.m., and 4:30 p.m. The food service CO was normally off work at 5 p.m. and didn't like to stay past that time. Also no inmate was allowed to get an early lunch (or dinner) and come again for a late lunch (or dinner).

Inmates with specific health or religious restrictions were given a special meal that was approved by the chaplain or the camp nurse. These meals were delivered frozen to their bunks in the camp. These inmates would leave the food on their desk to thaw out before they ate it. That food usually thawed out in a few hours. If the inmate didn't want special meals, vegetarian options ranged from cottage cheese to peanut butter and jelly sandwiches. However, inmates were not allowed to have both vegetarian and the special meals.

When I worked in food service, I served inmates as much as the CO on duty ordered. If he saw me give more, I could get in trouble. At the end of the meal, some COs would allow us to give out seconds and thirds. On chicken days, there were no seconds. I never understood why, however. Whether inmates received seconds would be determined by the CO. There were never seconds during the food service line.

Inmates made the food at the camp, but COs watched over them to make sure that it was made properly. When I was at food service, the CO stayed in the backroom. Some COs cooked and others stayed in the office.

There was several conspiracy theories that claimed the food was old or past the expiration date. On April 11, 2012, I had a bag of potato chips along with tuna or boiled eggs, potato salad, lettuce, and vegetable soup. The next day I found out that the chips' sell-by date was January 23, 2012, nearly four months before I ate them. I and several inmates did eat several bags of those chips.

Some inmates tried to maintain a diet for religious or health reasons. I chose not to worry about a diet because if the food service meals weren't healthy, neither was the food from the commissary list. I got Top Ramen noodles in from the commissary that had to be at least a month past the sell-by date. Some of the ready-made rice or beans had as much sodium as any bag of chips.

But the only real time the food was a problem for me was when cooks oversalted the food to their taste. I was very gassy most days, and I noticed that I used the bathroom more than when I was at home. Most inmates complained that the food increased their weight because of the salt and sugar content. I was holding a doubled-edged sword: either eat the food, which could be unhealthy, or try to survive off the small vegetarian meals. What was an inmate going do? It was all the food we had there. The food didn't taste too bad. It just wasn't fresh or great.

I didn't eat the fruit or vegetables because they weren't fresh and they didn't agree with my stomach. But the meat I could stomach enough to like. Most of the side dishes, such as the mashed potatoes and macaroni and cheese, were damn good or decent.

Some inmates claimed the COs put food meant for inmates in their cars. Other inmates put food in their lockers and traded it for commissary items. Usually it was the meat, eggs, or cheese that was stolen, but other food items were stolen as well. Most of the time, the inmate cooks would make sure each inmate had at least their fair share of food before stealing, while other inmates didn't care and sometimes we ran out of chicken, hamburger, or pork. Depending on the dish, some inmate cooks would make up for the missing food ingredients by using excessive amounts of pasta noodles, carrots, celery, or onions, sometimes even bread to make the food stretch, or to make it last longer. But what choice did they have? There were too many people who handled the food and there was little accountability for CO actions.

Rumor had it that the food was not made for human consumption. Inmates at the warehouse for food service claimed to have seen disclaimers on food boxes. I didn't see these labels nor would anyone give me proof of these claims.

Sometimes we got dishes made from MREs (meals ready to eat) served along with our meals, such as enchiladas or steaks. It might not have been the tastiest meal, but it felt good having extra food.

We stopped having regular breakfast on June 4, 2012. After that time, the camp and the FCI would serve continental breakfast instead of the normal breakfast.

Conspiracy theories flowing around said that the BOP was cutting the breakfast to get more people to pay for the commissary. There had been a lot of white-collars being admitted, whom many inmates believed had big money to spend. The influx of these criminals plus eliminating breakfast, some inmates believed, would force all inmates to buy commissary food, making more money for the prisons, admins, and COs. However, a lot of inmates didn't like the breakfast at camp and wanted food from the commissary because it tasted better and it was healthier. There were times when only six inmates were in line for breakfast.

Weekly Commissary Shopping

T he commissary was the prison camp grocery store. To buy from the commissary, we made our selections from a two-page list of products ranging from snacks to hair products to batteries to greeting cards. I have no idea where the commissary received their products. I've heard a ton of rumors, such as the products were donated from business or the BOP purchased them, but I can't prove these rumors.

All inmates had to turn their lists in by ten in the morning on Tuesday to get the items wanted on Wednesday. Because my first day at camp was on a Thursday, I couldn't get my commissary items until the following Wednesday.

On the list, there were two stereos. The first one, which cost $40, was an AM/FM radio with five preset buttons, cheap headphones, and a clock. The second cost about $24 and had no preset buttons, headphones, or clock. I took the $40 one because I figured I could use it as a radio and clock, since I didn't wear watches at home anyway. Both radios were specially manufactured and had a transparent case to make it easy for COs to see if the radio was damaged in any way.

Most of the snacks were food that lasted a long time, like chips, sodas, ramen noodles, and seasonings. Ice cream was also available, but it had to be eaten quickly because there was no place to store it. Inmates were not allowed to have any coolers of any kind in their lockers.

Along with normal commissary items, there were special deals and clearance items that were only available that day or month. Inmates purchased limited-edition Nikes or other name-brand shoes. I didn't care too much for those shoes because they were as much as $50 and more. One inmate, who I'll call Fake Pastor, told me he bought a pair of $100 shoes. He had about ten pairs in his bunk. A few other inmates did the same.

The $70 I put on my books when I first came to camp went quick, and I ended up getting more money sent in. The first week I spent $140 on the basics: shaving cream, radio, headphones, snacks, hygiene, and sweats. One brother hooked me up with a pair of sweatpants and a sweatshirt for $40. It would have cost me almost $30 otherwise. I paid him back in tuna and stamps.

Once I got into the swing of things, I only brought stamps, tuna, Top Ramen, Magic Shave, and an occasional snack. At first I bought weekly, but soon I bought for the month, and only when I felt that I needed it.

I avoided sodas and candies because they reminded me of home. I also didn't like the price of $3.70 for an eight-pack. I drank the juice from the cafeteria or just had water. I wasn't going to be there too long so I didn't want to get too comfortable. I just wanted enough stuff to get through the experience.

Plus, there was always a way to get free powder fruit juice from work, by winning awards, or from other inmates.

Exercise and Recreation Room

One of the first rooms an inmate saw after walking into the administrative building was the exercise room. That room had the stair climbers, bikes, and treadmills—with no electrical equipment, as explained earlier. There was also a TV with a remote and cable. There was also a TV/DVD hookup in a storage room within the rec room along with the sporting equipment, guitars, and books about music. Inmates needed permission to get sporting equipment, but we didn't need it for the guitars or books.

Inmates could watch TV while exercising. However, the first inmate there would jump on the comfortable bike and do just enough to exercise while watching whatever he wanted on television. There was a supply room behind the exercise room with another television, no cable, and just a DVD. It was a thirty-inch or forty-inch TV like the one in the exercise room.

Most of the inmates didn't blast the television, out of respect for the admins, whose offices were next door, and for fear of losing the television. However, about a month before I left, the television in the exercise room was removed because inmates started playing loud rap music on the TV, annoying the admins.

The television in the back, however, had a ton of

DVDs that we called the leisure library. Inmates would take DVDs from the library and not return them. To keep them in the leisure library, I hid a few of my favorite DVDs in a witchcraft DVD jacket, then put it back on the leisure library's shelves just so I could have them when I needed them. I knew no one would touch the witchcraft CDs because so many inmates thought it was satanic. Other inmates hid DVDs in religious books knowing that no one would look there.

However, I avoided the back room because contrabands were always found there and the room might be locked by COs at any given time. If it was locked, inmates had to ask COs to unlock it. It was a pain to get a CO to move if he didn't feel like doing anything. Plus, there was no desk in the back room, making it difficult to write.

Exercising in Prison Camp

One of the best ways to release stress was to work out daily. Exercise helped get out any anger I had as well as getting my blood circulating and giving me a break from the library. The camp didn't have an official workout program. They would encourage inmates to work out in their leisure time. Inmates would create workout schedules and workout groups to help reach their needs and goals.

We did a lot of cardio, stretching, and calisthenics for our exercise routine.

Inmates at this prison were banned from using weights. Weights were defined as anything an inmate could use to add weight to their workout. If an inmate put pounds of dirt in a box or sandbag, then bench-pressed it, that box or bag would be considered a weight. The mere sight of sandbags would get an inmate sent to the SHU (solitary housing unit) and/or the room or area the contraband was found in would be locked or closed off.

I was told by an inmate that since 2004, no prisons could have weights. One story claimed that inmates got too strong and beat up COs. Another story was that inmates beat each other up with them. Who knows, they are probably both true.

However, that's not to say weights didn't exist in camp. I worked out with some people and pulled a thigh muscle because I lifted more than I could handle. Of course, if I went to the nurse's office she could have told a CO I was lifting weights, and that CO could have sent me to the hole, or SHU, to await my punishment. In all likelihood, I would have received a shot (gotten disciplined) and it could have resulted in grief for the camp inmates. I had to just tough it out for two weeks.

I only worked out sparingly the first few weeks. Once I started working eight hours a day, I didn't want to work out because I wanted to get as much studying and writing done as possible.

Once I quit the powerhouse, I worked out about five times a week and as much as two hours a day. I even got up to a full hour on the treadmill and improved my time working out a ton.

I weighed as much as 196 pounds when I got there. I had dropped to 180 pounds by a few weeks before I left.

I had a workout buddy who put me through a light workout. My workouts weren't that crazy. They would include ten dips, five pull-ups, twenty push-ups, twenty sit-ups, and a hundred-yard sprint. I'd do about six sets, then jog for thirty minutes to an hour. Sometimes, we'd use jumping jacks or mountain climbers to mix up the exercises.

I saw some inmates working out until it hurt. There were a few inmates who were chiseled like a statue. Those inmates did two workouts a day for over an hour each. My second workout was yoga.

Talking to Admins

The first case manager I had was a very stressed-out person. Either she was super lazy or she was very stressed. Some Blacks felt she gave Whites more halfway house time and more furloughs. Other Blacks told me that more Whites had homes and families that were more likely to be approved for furloughs by the probation officers. By the same token, a lot of Blacks didn't have those qualifications for one reason or another. Maybe they had a history of crime in their family or the living environment wouldn't be approved. The Blacks also felt she favored Whites and Mexicans for community service projects because of their work ethic. I honestly couldn't see the possibly of her being racist. But she hated her job with a passion. She quit, or retired, to help her family.

I hated going to the first case manager's office. She was kind of cool, but if I stuttered, she would snap, "Get it out." I thought it was rude and annoying, but I had to bite my tongue. Her presence even bugged me.

It was about the eighth month of my sentence when I heard rumors about a new case manager. The inmates got optimistic. Some short-term inmates felt they were going to get additional halfway house time and furloughs. While other long-term inmates didn't remotely care, I was in the "wait and see" camp.

The case manager finally came in my ninth month. To my shock it was a Black lady. She was from Herlong's medium-security prison camp. The majority of the Blacks had long sentences so it really didn't matter to them. However, some of the white-collar Blacks felt they were going to get hooked up by her. I was still in my wait and see mode because, as I told someone, "I met a person who was Black and he was more racist to us than Whites." I actually was afraid she was going to screw us over more than the first case manager just to make sure there were no signs of favoritism.

It turned out that she was firm but favorable. She even tried to hook me up with more halfway house time and a furlough. As I explain in the community service chapter, I couldn't get additional halfway house time. As far as the furlough, she promised me a five-day furlough, but during my community service it was reduced to three days because either someone read the books wrong or the warden changed the rules. I honestly heard both stories. Plus, my family would have to pay all travel expenses to and from the camp, which was out of my parents' price range. Being that I was less than six months away from coming home, it wasn't worth it.

One day, the second case manager was talking to me about the yoga teacher. I answered her questions but I really didn't give her any real personality behind it. I just wanted her to hurry up and leave.

She asked me, "Do I seem standoffish to you? Some inmates think I'm hard to talk to so they can't be themselves."

I shook my head. "No. it's not you. It's me. I'm very standoffish. Please don't take it personal." She gave me a weird look, and I walked away. After that conversation, I kept my distance from her, as she did me.

During my time there, I saw two secretaries who assisted the case manager and the other admins. I don't remember the first secretary at all. However, the second one arrived with optimism. She felt like she was going to change the prison camp and culture with love and compassion. Three weeks later, she became the irate employee who hated her job and was stuck at it. After my community service job, I noticed that the new secretary was recruiting inmates for community service projects. I don't know if the case manager or the warden assigned the task to the secretary. However, after my experience with the community project, I refused to ever do it again. After I repeatedly rejected her offers to do community service, she became cold and standoffish to me. I could tell it annoyed her when I told her no and got away with it. I think most of those admins didn't like inmates saying no, for some reason.

The camp counselor was very cool to me because I gave him the utmost respect and didn't bug him. I only talked to him when I needed something or he addressed me. Unlike other inmates, I didn't try to get the latest information or find out the truth behind the rumors from him, because I knew that annoyed him. Also, I wasn't sure if he was telling the truth about those things. The inmates would get so much false information, or get the information wrong, I started to believe the counselor or other admins were feeding them wrong information.

I had to go to him to get out of the powerhouse. At first, I wanted to be an orderly, but he told me no way. He didn't give a reason, but YT and I believe it was because he might have thought I wanted to be lazy. He made it clear to me that he picked his orderly, and no one else. He never gave a reason. I just accepted it. But when I told him I had an approval to go to food service, he signed it almost immediately. He was very quick-witted and sarcastic to inmates who pushed his buttons. To me, he was direct with only a hint of sarcasm. Maybe he respected me. I honestly have no idea.

When I saw him at the lunch lines, I said nothing to him, or to any of the other officers or admins. One time he told me to make sure I got rid of a cardboard box I had from a pair of boots I just got. All he said was, "Be sure to get rid of that box when you get situated."

I said, "Yes, sir," and that was that. I don't even remember him cussing at me like he would other inmates who whined or pushed his buttons. He embarrassed other inmates with his dry wit and sarcasm.

Correctional Officers

O verall, the COs didn't bother me. Even the so-called assholes left me alone. All they wanted was to sit around and do nothing. There would be two COs in charge at any one time. There was the food service CO, who left at 5:00 p.m., and the one in charge of the camp. There would be four different camp COs every day, each one on a different shift. The camp COs would usually rotate every three months. During those three months, the COs would take vacations regularly and would be replaced by COs from the FCI. If no COs from the FCI were available, then one of the admins would act as camp CO.

Overall I got respect from a lot of the COs because I just let them do their job, and my bunky NB was well-respected among them. They saw me writing and walking around with books. They saw me in the library or working out all day. They knew I didn't want any trouble.

A few COs that stood out were the ones in the food service area. Ms. Roberta and Ms. Sara were two of my favorite female COs. Both COs were in the food service area. Ms. Roberta was a sweetheart. She always tried to hook inmates up with extra foods that they liked, rather than more veggies or desserts or MREs, because she knew inmates didn't eat those foods. Ms. Sara didn't care about her job, and she did just enough to get the job done and not get fired. She was super laid-back and always joked with us.

Ms. Lisa was in charge of the dorms in the afternoon. She split her time between being the main camp CO and a food service CO. As I mentioned before, she was cool to me. However, she was ghetto, and most inmates loved it. I guess it reminded them of their girls at home.

Another CO was called Horse Face by the inmates. She had a nice body, for a CO, but a face like a horse. She gave inmates an attitude when we wanted her to do anything that involved her leaving her office. Her job, like the other COs', was to make sure the libraries and other rooms were available for inmate use, usually by 6:00 a.m. Instead, we would have to wait until almost eight in the morning. Because asking her several times would only annoy her and telling the admins might result in possible retaliation, I would just patiently wait for an older inmate to talk to her. Somehow, they had a way to politely get their way with COs without getting in trouble or snitching.

Some male COs would come into the library to sit and talk to us. Some gave us breath tests just to make sure that we were not drinking. Other COs would take the DVD players out for inmates to watch in other rooms or the barbershop.

Once in a while, we would get COs who dug in the baseball diamond or the sage fields to see if they could find contraband. They usually found contraband. I didn't know if a snitch told on other inmates or if they just randomly checked. In any case, inmates hid stuff in the same places every time.

There was one CO named Santiago who was always picking on certain inmates because he knew that he could get a reaction.

Then there was Biff. He was the most childish CO ever. He broke one of the Gators, the golf carts inmates and COs used to travel throughout the camp, by trying to do jumps on the small dirt hills in the fields. Rumor had it he was banned from using the Gators. One time, Biff put a bunch of milk cartons under an inmate's mattress because he found them in that inmate's locker. When the inmate lay on his bed, he crushed the milk cartons, and milk poured all over the inmate's square. Biff must have figured it was better to pull a prank on the inmate instead of giving him a shot. However, Biff only picked on inmates who whined about being in camp or who snitched on him. He would make dumb offensive remarks to inmates. White-collar inmates complained about his actions. When there was something they didn't like, inmates sent a cop-out, or a Request to Administrator Form, to complain about other inmates, COs, and admins, or to request to talk to an admin. The inmate would address complaint forms to the camp counselor or the camp administrator, and they would either address the problem or totally ignore it. In this particular case, the camp administration and the lieutenant punished Biff, but I have no idea what his punishment entailed. However, Biff retaliated by locking doors or doing a random locker search of the inmates who told on him. That was why inmates told me never to tell on COs, because those inmates got it worse.

Sometimes, I thought that some of the COs were lightweight sadists because they used their powers to please or thrill themselves. We all had to stand up for the 10 p.m. count. Sometimes we were dead asleep, but we still had to get up and put both feet on the ground. The count might not start until 10:15 or 10:30, and it lasted for fifteen minutes. It was a pain to have to stand up when I had to be at work at 7 a.m. I just reminded myself that it was prison, not paradise.

The COs would take count seriously, and I was never sure why. If we messed up their count, we would get retaliation or sent to the SHU. One day during the 4 p.m. count, Fake Pastor didn't want to stand up because he was sleeping. The CO, let's call him Billy Bob, got pissed and took it personally.

When I came back from serving the dinner lines, I saw Billy Bob pulling out everything from Fake Pastor's locker and his bunky's locker. Technically, he was searching for contraband, but he just pulled everything out and examined it.

That same night, I was in the library when I heard "yard recall" on the intercom, which meant that all camp inmates had to return to the barracks immediately.

Once inside, we had a bed book count. I stood by my bunk. When the two officers came, I said my last name and registration number. One CO read my name from the binder which had copies of all the inmate IDs in it. The other CO checked out my ID before he moved to the next square. It was time-consuming but not longer than the regular count.

Billy Bob then gave a profanity-laced rant to everyone about how we needed to stand for count. He reminded us how lucky we were as campers and that we needed to stop being stupid. "Stand up for count. Both feet on the floor." Then he did a regular count and walked outside with two other officers while we remained standing at our bunks. Five minutes later, he came back in and said, "Clear." That was to punish us for moving when the count wasn't clear and for Fake Pastor sleeping in count.

Technically, we were supposed to stand at our bunks until the CO said "clear." However, some COs didn't yell clear. They just went into their office, and we assumed it meant that we're good. Of course, there were a few inmates who would stand for a second just to be counted and sit down. I usually leaned against the bedpost with both feet on the floor, and my bunky sat on his bed until he needed to stand. No way was I going to go on my top bunk during count.

Next day, we all joked about what happened the day before. I was in the classroom when Billy Bob walked through and announced, "Camp recall, emergency count." I went into the barracks and it was silent. There were four officers, Billy Bob and three others, with stern looks on their faces. We could tell that one of these people was a lieutenant because he had a white shirt instead of the normal blue.

"Bed book count, and I better hear some numbers!" Billy Bob said.

The officers came down my row first. Just as the officers passed my bunk, an officer said, "I'm not telling you fuckers again, IDs out!"

After half of the barracks was counted, the lieutenant told that half to sit down. The officers finished the count while scolding three inmates for sitting down without his permission.

Then the lieutenant gave a profane rant, telling us that if we wanted "that sweet living" we better do our part and do as we were told. We were also threatened with daily piss testing, extended bed book counts, locker searches, and COs coming through trying to raise hell.

I heard one officer say, "Aren't we supposed to have a fire drill?" The other officers said, "Yeah, yeah." Then, for the first time in two years, we had a fire drill.

We stood outside ten to fifteen minutes in twenty-degree weather. Billy Bob said, "This is a fire drill. This is the only fucking time you use the back door. Now, get in a single-file line and I'm counting you as you come in. If you've been in the military you know what a single-file line is. I don't want a clusterfuck."

Once back inside, we stood at our bunks until they yelled clear and got out of sight. At which point, the inmates made fun of the officers.

Then there was Mr. Purple. Mr. Purple came to supervise the food service area for a few weeks. The first time I met him, he introduced himself by saying, "I'm by the book." I understood that to mean that he followed the policy laid out in the inmate and CO handbook. Some inmates found that all COs didn't really go by the book as much as they went by their personal interpretation of the book.

Mr. Purple didn't allow us to wear hats in the food service area. Not to mention, we had to enter the area from the far door. He only allowed food service workers into the short line. These rules were not regularly enforced. However, after Purple left, I noticed that the rule was enforced more.

He reposted a memo that reminded inmates not to feed the birds or we could get three 300-series shots and an automatic trip to the hole. (A 300-series infraction was pretty moderate. If you did something really bad you could get a 200- or 100-series shot.) The memo was posted in five places through the camp and was torn down as soon as Mr. Purple was off shift. His reason for not feeding the birds was to not get sea gull poop everywhere. Most inmates believed he was power tripping and fed the birds when he wasn't looking.

Mr. Purple claimed he was going to fix inmates' hours and help food service COs with their roster for both morning and night crews. For some reason, those things never happened. According to the rumors, the system shut down and the other food service COs had to fix the system. He was supposed to be there for two weeks for a total of six night shifts and six day shifts. Instead, he was only there for six shifts total. I have no idea what happened to him.

Billy Bob and Lisa hated the inmates' using the back door. The only approved reason for using the backdoor was during emergencies, like fires. Other than that, COs, the case manager, and the counselor didn't want the door open. The problem with the back door was that inmates would sneak out to get their cell phones and contrabands to and from the baseball diamond. I saw a few inmates get shots for using the door when the camp counselor was on duty. They didn't want it opened because they couldn't see the inmates from their office. However, we had a number of COs who didn't care if the back door was used or not. As long as they could sit in their office and go online or listen to their radio, they didn't care what we did with the back door.

Then we would get COs like Turtle, who was another total jerk. First, he woke up the camp at 6:05 a.m. I have never heard of a CO doing that, but it wasn't a problem since I was already out of bed. Twenty minutes later, he announced over the intercom that if we had any extra laundry, especially sheets and pillows, that we were to get rid of them or he would take them. I had hidden my extra pillows. I had two of them on an empty bunk on the freeway. Other inmates washed their sheets to hide the extra ones they had.

Turtle walked up and down, starting with the freeway around 7:10 a.m., slamming boxes and chairs and collecting any laundry. I lost my extra pillow, and a few people lost their extra blankets and pillows.

Throughout his shift, he searched lockers, dumped out weights made by inmates from buckets or boxes of dirt near the baseball diamond, and searched every room. He got irate because there were too many people washing blankets. Some inmates washed them over and over, I guess trying to keep them in the washing machine until his shift ended at 2 p.m.

He called an emergency count then ordered us to get our chairs out of the TV room and any extra chairs out from out of bounds. Afterward he walked through with another CO and did a bed book count. We were cleared, and seconds later all the warehouse workers were called back and another bed book count was done. A standup count followed, but Turtle was counting by himself.

He finished his one-man count and then shouted, "There is no one here to do this count so someone else is going to do it. You can move around the dorm, but you can't leave."

To be honest, it really didn't make too much sense because he shouldn't have done a count unless a second CO helped him. I just shrugged it off like the other inmates did.

Minutes later, the camp counselor entered the dorm and demanded a count. He made the whole place silent by threatening to send folks to the hole for talking and making any noise during count. They did two quick back-to-back counts then put us on camp lockdown, which meant we could walk in the dorm but couldn't go outside it.

The counselor locked the leisure library and the barbershop, and cut off access to the classroom and multipurpose room. We got access to the rooms the next day. Turtle never came back during my time there.

I later found out that there was a fire in the SHU so they had to do several counts to make sure that the campers didn't escape. The prison camp officials believed that camp inmates might escape from the camp because COs would be distracted. However, camp inmates were not surrounded by fences and no CO would chase a camp inmate if he wanted to escape. Needless to say, I'm still confused to this day about why they thought we were all going to make a break for it.

Meetings with Camp Officials

Every meeting that I attended at Herlong FPC felt as if I was supposed to just stand there while they talked. If I had permission, I could talk later. I always felt as if I was pretty low, but to minimize my time there I did the best that I could to keep the conversations short and to the point.

During my second day at camp, I had my first meeting with the camp counselor. It was a brief conversation about the rules of the camp. He said he'd tell me more when I had the admissions and orientation meeting a few weeks later. That meeting was quick because I just filled out a few pieces of paper and left.

My first meeting with the case manager was on my third day of camp, and it felt rushed. She was very stressed, and it seemed as if she had a lot on her plate. I don't know if she hated her job, hated inmates, or hated non-Whites. There were rumors of all three.

She asked me questions about my education, work experience, and family life. After what seemed like fifty questions, she gave me a printed copy of my answers. She asked me about my plans after prison. When I told her I was going to be a blogger and writer, she said, "That's not realistic. You should work at the powerhouse or GM6 to get a trade." She went on, claiming that writers don't make a lot of money and that it was her job to make sure that I got the skills needed to prevent coming back to prison.

That meeting was a shocker. I came into camp thinking I'd get six months in a halfway house in Sacramento. The case manager said that there was no halfway house in Sacramento and the amount of halfway that she gave out was 10 percent of the sentence, according to the Bureau of Prisons policy. According to the report in front of me, I was only going to get fifty-four days of halfway house time. I had planned on going back to my old restaurant job, unless I could prevent it with a trade. However, because there was no halfway house in Sacramento it would be difficult to go back to that job. In addition, the longer I was gone from the job, the harder it would be to get re-hired.

I was told by my lawyer that my good behavior time would be based on the 27 months of my original sentence, or roughly 2.7 months off. However, I only got 1.7 months off because it was based on the 17 months I had to serve. I voiced my opinion about it, but it didn't matter. I figured that was fine, I got the sentence reduction so it didn't matter.

Around June 2011, which was about a month after I got there, I attended my first admissions and orientation meeting. The A&O meeting was my orientation to prison and its policies and programs. We had to watch a rape prevention tape. During the meeting, we were told about each type of officer that we might interact with while there. They included the camp nurse, GED teacher, psychologist, and the COs for maintenance, food service, recreation, and barracks.

We talked to the camp counselor, who had been in the system for over twenty-five years and didn't give a fuck about shit. He was a sarcastic hard-ass who lived to "make it hurt" when inmates got in trouble.

The officer in charge of giving us disciplinary actions, such as additional time or fines, came primarily to warn us about what happened when we saw him. I'll call him Daly. We only saw Daly if we were in a lot of trouble.

Repeatedly the officers and counselor would mention the term *shot*. A shot is any documented disciplinary action resulting from an inmate's actions. There are four levels of shots, with the least severe being the 400 series, and the 100 series being the most severe. Each level might carry additional disciplinary actions as well as loss of privileges such as receiving mail, using TRUL-INCS, or purchasing from the commissary, whatever Daly deemed suitable for our actions. Usually a 100 series shot would cause a loss of several privileges, time in the SHU, and possible transfer to another prison or camp. The SHU (also known as the solitary housing unit or the hole or solitary confinement) was a set of cells separate from the camp population that could have as many as two inmates in it.

Usually a 400 series shot is a warning, and maybe a loss of a privilege of the camp administrators' or lieutenants' choosing. However, in theory, if Daly felt an inmate was a security risk, that inmate could be transferred to another prison or stay in the SHU. To my knowledge, Daly would listen to camp admins for advice for what would be best for the inmate and the security of the camp.

I didn't even care about any of what they presented in A&O. Most of the information was presented so fast that I couldn't get it all. I did get one thing from it all, however. Don't mess up or these guys will enjoy punishing you, and don't bug them unless it's important to the CO. To be honest, that's all I really needed to know.

I had another meeting with the case manager about my halfway house time. Because my sentence was so short, I had to get my paperwork for the halfway house done sooner than later. At that meeting I found out that I had ninety days of halfway house time and I would be leaving the camp on May 7, 2012. I asked why I couldn't get six months of halfway house time. Her answer was because I had a strong family at home who would be able to help me, I didn't need as much government assistance as other inmates. She went on to say that the halfway house closest to Sacramento was in Oakland. She then said I would have to get on home confinement when I got to the halfway house if I wanted to make Sacramento my home. There was no other assistance she was willing to give me.

I asked her about the possibility of getting a furlough. I was thinking that I could use the furlough to get my old job back or to figure out apartment information in Sacramento to get ahead of the game before I got to the halfway house. She told me that the warden only gave furloughs to inmates who did community service. I had to be at the camp for six months before I was eligible for community service. At the time of that meeting, I'd been there for less than two months. I just figured that somehow things would work themselves out in the end; they always did.

Prison Camp Programming

One of the most important things an inmate needed to do was prepare for his post-prison life. The BOP felt that inmates needed to focus on becoming educated, learning employment skills, and enjoying leisure time to be a well-rounded citizen. Doing this would reduce prison camp violence and reduce the likelihood of inmates returning to crime. According to the Code of Federal Regulations, section 544.80, Purpose and Scope, "In consideration of inmate education, occupation, and leisure-time needs, the Bureau of Prisons affords inmates the opportunity to improve their knowledge and skills through academic, occupation and leisure-time activities. All institutions, except satellite camps, detention centers and metropolitan correctional centers, shall operate a full range of activities as outlined in this rule."

The programming at Herlong Prison Camp was very minimal because it was a satellite of FCI Herlong. Some of the programming was taught or lead by prison camp faculty. The GED teacher taught the GED programs and any higher educational programs with Lassen College. The chaplain presided over the weekly religious service and a sixteen-week lifestyle course, called threshold program, that was designed to help inmates deal with prison and adjust to the real world. Programming also came in the form of working at a job. Working in the food service department or cutting hair as a barber counted as programming. Doing community service work also was seen as programming.

Most of the programming happened when an inmate joined classes taught by other inmates. At the camp, we had inmates who taught yoga, others who taught religious beliefs as well as arts and crafts. When YT taught the yoga classes, he got high praise from the admins. Also any inmate who exercised, read books, or wrote in a journal could ask for that activity to be considered programming. All they would have to do was turn in their program to the case manager, who would assign either the multipurpose room, crafts room, or classroom 2 for the class and would post a schedule for the rooms in the library and multipurpose room.

When those rooms were not used, camp inmates would work out, play instruments, or study. Because the schedule could cause misunderstandings and conflicts and interruptions in classes, some friends of the scheduled instructor's class would schedule classes during their friend's time slot if they knew that instructor wasn't going to make it.

The threshold program was a program to help inmates readjust in society by helping them with life skills such as basic budgeting, how to talk to employers, how to talk to family, and how to be open and honest with himself to be a better man.

I understood that all people taking the class did was go off-subject and complain about prison policies and used it as an excuse to talk to the chaplain, who was running the classes weekly. Everyone I talked to about the class didn't like it at all. They just took the class to show proof that they were programming.

The community service was considered programming. My writing in the library was considered programming. Working at the powerhouse and working in food service was considered programming. Taking classes at Lassen College was considered programming.

However, I felt that the programming was about meeting the admins' and COs' quotas and proving to the American public that the prison was attempting to help the inmates while putting the blame for inmates' post-prison success squarely on the inmate. A lot of the time inmates didn't learn anything at their jobs or schooling, yet they were forced to go because they had to prove that they were trying to change. Also the jobs helped keep the camp and FCI functional and self-sustaining by using cheap labor to repair equipment and feed inmates and avoid the high cost of professionals such as repairmen or caterers. Also GED classes were a way to get additional funding for the camp. The more inmates in GED classes, the more the federal government would fund the camp. I'm not sure how or where the money was given, however.

Programming in camp did little to instill confidence in inmates at the camp. I can't speak about the FCI because I wasn't there. The COs and admins in charge of these programs were too busy with other job duties or didn't see a point in teaching their programming classes, so they would go through the motions and rush the classes along. That led many of the camp inmates to feel they didn't get the skills needed to prevent returning to prison. I've even heard some inmates planning on returning to correctional faculties because they didn't see any future for themselves. The reason I was confident about my post-prison life was because of my degree and the skills I'd already proven to myself.

Working at the Powerhouse

Every inmate at Herlong worked unless he somehow got fired at every single job and there was nowhere he could work. Of these jobs, the powerhouse was one of the jobs inmates wanted the most. The powerhouse was a department supervised by COs and led by inmates that focused on repairing the electric, HVAC, and water systems at the camp and the FCI. We repaired the breakers, air conditioners, heaters, and boilers, and maintained the sewer systems, and checked the quality of the waters. Once in a while, we would help other departments, but it was rare.

The powerhouse was located about a mile from the camp and a few feet from the side entrance of the FCI. It was in a plazalike setting with separate buildings for GM6, Unicor, and the warehouse. GM6, or General Maintenance 6, was the department of inmates who repaired the camp and prison vehicles. They would also do landscaping, welding, and structural repairs. They were the ones who built the handball wall, soccer goals, and the basketball hoops.

The Unicor building was where inmates used to work for Unicor. Unicor was a manufacturer of furniture and supplies for the military, the prison, and merchants and retailers. However, when I arrived the Unicor building was used to store supplies for the other inmates. I was told that Unicor was shut down due to poor management and inmates creating a poor product.

During my first week at camp I got the job at the powerhouse because of another inmate. Frank, a forty-three-year-old Black man, had worked at the powerhouse for over a year. He was an unofficial mentor to me. He was doing what I wanted to do, which was to work my butt off to get as much education as possible so I could get a good job when I was released. He told me he worked at the powerhouse because they were going to have classes in HVAC and boilers. I was also told that we could also get certifications in various trades by working a certain amount of hours after the powerhouse COs felt we were ready. I figured it was a great way to gain a trade to avoid working in the restaurant industry and to have a better-paying job until my writing projects become profitable.

The first day at work was about the beginning of June 2011, and it went by very fast. After breakfast, I would go back to the dorm and wait until 7:00 a.m. to walk down to the powerhouse. I walked with twenty or so other inmates down the same road that led to the GM6, powerhouse, and warehouse departments. Once I arrived at the powerhouse, I would wait until the COs arrived. They were supposed to arrive at 7:30 a.m., but sometimes they would be late and we would have to wait until we were told to leave. Normally, Frank or another inmate lead would check with the other departments to find out where the COs were.

At the powerhouse I was re-introduced to all the

COs. Brasher and Shaw had been COs for over fourteen years. They had experience in construction work and were journeymen electricians. Lannom was a career CO with no trade experience outside the camp. The three took that job because they wanted a steady paycheck and the medical and retirement benefits were excellent. I was sent with an inmate named Luthor to work in the grinding station, which was the sewage station for the FCI and the FPC.

We drove to the grinding station, which was on the right side of the FCI, in a Gator. Luthor opened the side door, which was opened by the powerhouse COs before they arrived at the powerhouse. Afterward, he brought up a large garage door and drove the Gator inside the building.

The first thing I noticed was that it smelled like sewage and old garbage. Because I've worked as a janitor at Walmart, I was used to those smells, and sights for that matter. There were four garbage cans in a square with a metal sheet on top of the cans. Above the cans was a massive tube called an augur that dumped sewage and garbage into the garbage cans. Behind the cans was a chest-high guardrail that went several feet back, where it connected to a flight of stairs on the left and a control panel on the right. The stairs led down to the sewage system.

The system had two routes, one going to the grinder. The grinder ground the sewage and garbage until it could flow through the auger without clogging it. From the auger, it would drop into the garbage cans. When the garbage cans were full, we would empty them.

The second route went to Herlong's sewage system, which was monitored by FCI Herlong Sewer Treatment Services. Our job was to prevent large items of garbage from going into Herlong's sewage systems or the auger and grinder. If large garbage went into the grinder or auger, it would stop the machine from working. That meant more sewage would go to Lassen County sewage, and the powerhouse COs would get in trouble by their bosses. In turn, Luthor and I would get cussed out, and we might receive disciplinary actions as well.

The control panel controlled the auger and the grinder. We only touched those controls when we needed to stop a large piece of garbage from going up the grinder or we were cleaning it. I've seen it all, shit, pee, toilet paper, shirts, chips, bedding, stuffing from the bedding. It all went down the massive tube. Luthor told me that he saw dope, weapons, and other contrabands when the FCI had shakedowns. During the time that I was there, I didn't see any contraband.

My next job was to blow away all the excess sand around the main building with a leaf blower. Some of the sand couldn't be removed with the blower so I had to use a shovel. After about twenty minutes of shoveling dirt, Frank came out and started helping me. He told me that I was working too hard and that he couldn't let me do that work by myself. He then complained that people should be more helpful. I listened to him, but I really didn't care. I was just trying to stay busy and prove my worth. Once we were done, we drove back to the camp and had lunch at about 11:30 a.m.

After lunch, Frank taught me a little about the boilers

and how they read the gauges. I also learned how to take water samples from the FCI. As he was teaching me, one of the powerhouse COs, Shaw, jumped in and started teaching me and talked about his experience with doing that type of work in the civilian world.

Before I knew it, it was 2:15 p.m. and the COs allowed us to go back to the camp. Once I got out of the shower and changed, I started reading books about how to get an electrician's license and HVAC certification. I even talked to my mom about ordering these books so I could learn while I was there.

The next day, after I finished the sewer with Luthor, I took a few water samples. Frank hooked me up in the powerhouse because he believed that I was a good reader. He put me in the back where I tested the water for the camp and the FCI. I just needed to make sure that the pH levels were correct and that the chemicals were not out of balance. I charted my results on a paper and put it in the notebook with several months of results and paperwork. After that, I added salt in the container to soften the hard water in the camp and the FCI. I did that once a week. Next, I checked all of the meters and gauges of the boilers to make sure they hadn't gotten too high during the night.

Once I was done with that, the COs made the whole crew pull weeds around a water tower that was just outside the prison complex. A building next to the water tower helped clean the water before it came into the camp and the FCI. The water tower collected the water. From there the water went into the pipes that went inside the neighboring building, then into the camp. There was usually a ton of weeds around these buildings. Because the powerhouse was responsible for that area, we had to pull the weeds when we had time.

I was pretty quiet at the job. I asked questions but avoided a lot of personal conversation and joking. I just wanted to get a feel for the people there and to keep everyone out of my business. I studied as much about the systems as possible and stayed on top of my responsibilities. When I ran out of things to do, I would jump in the Gator and go see if Frank or one of the other inmates needed help. If not I would come back and see if the COs wanted me to do any special projects or find something to study. Those special projects would include cleaning the inmate and officer restrooms, sweeping the powerhouse, or whatever they came up with. One CO told me I had two weeks to get a sense of humor, mainly to make his job more interesting. It took me about three weeks. Then I was the butt of all the jokes, all in fun, of course.

During the next few months at the powerhouse, the only thing that made that job worth my time was the fact that time moved faster, which made my sentence seem shorter. I did a lot of studying for these trades, but the low pay made it difficult to want to keep working there. The crew was never larger than seven men when I was there. In fact, when I quit the powerhouse, it was down to four men. There was the normal drama and childishness, as in any other job, but overall it was very laid-back.

The starting pay for inmates at camp was $5 a month, which was called the maintenance pay. That pay was mainly for food service workers who didn't want to work long hours. For all other inmates, the pay started at $0.12 an hour for working as a grade 4, grade 3 was $0.17 an hour, grade 2 was $0.24 an hour, and grade 1 was $0.40 an hour plus an automatic 50 percent bonus for being the "lead guy." The only way an inmate got above a grade 4 was if the inmate had proof of a high school diploma or GED. My bachelor's degree in English did not satisfy that requirement because the government needed proof that I graduated from high school. The reason I was given was because the computer system my case manager used didn't have an option for my degree. Those who couldn't show proof of a GED or diploma had to take GED classes daily, regardless of their work schedule. I made it to grade 2. Sometimes one of the powerhouse COs, Lannom, who was in charge of our payroll, would give me 50 percent more because I worked hard.

The budget for the powerhouse, at least when I was there, provided enough money for two grade 1's, two grade 2's and several grade 3's and grade 4's. However, when I first started, they hired me as a grade 4, along with two other people. There were also two more people who were grade 3's. Once I had proof of my GED, I was given a raise to grade 3. After several inmates quit or went to Mendoza, I got a grade 2 raise. But that had a lot to do with some help I got from other inmates, and my work ethic was great. I didn't start any drama and I was eager to learn.

Throughout the camp, I had seen proof that poor work pay resulted in poor work performance. Projects would be half-assed or done just good enough to please the bosses. Some inmates wanted to work on themselves by making business plans for when they got out, developing their spiritual growth, or taking college classes, so they took the jobs with the fewest number of hours. Others were just lazy and didn't want to work at all. However, at the powerhouse, most of the workers worked their tail off because they enjoyed working hard and they wanted time to go by faster. Other inmates wanted to keep learning and working to keep their minds busy.

I never got above a grade 2 because I quit after five months at the job during the month of December 2011. I wouldn't have got a grade 1 anyway because I wasn't going to work there that long because of my sentence. A lot of inmates didn't want to work because the wages were too low. Many times there wasn't a lot of work, which was another reason that inmates sat around. I followed Frank, who always had something to do or instructed me to do something. If there was nothing to do, I'd find something to clean.

I would help Frank or whoever needed help. I helped fix a stove that was broken in the food service area. I was more of an assistant or a trainee, so I mainly held the tools and got whatever tools or parts Frank or whoever needed. I helped with replacing the AC units in the camp.

Frank was very hard-working and took a lot of pride in fixing anything in the camp that he could. According to him, the government probably wouldn't fix any broken appliance or machine. He, along with the other inmates, would be in danger of not eating or having no heat in the winter. Where other inmates would sit and complain about problems, he saw himself as fixing the problem. Honestly, it was hard to disagree with him.

Frank bailed me out during my fourth month at the powerhouse, around October 2011, when Brasher and Lannom scolded me and my grinding partner because shredded clothes and plastic items went into the city sewers. Over the next two days, Brasher questioned our work ethics and watched us work in the grinding station. Even with him watching us, items were still found in the city sewers, resulting in the city scolding him, and him scolding us. Finally Frank talked to Brasher and discovered the items didn't come from the prison camp, but they came from an area me and my partner didn't have access to. Brasher gave us an apology.

Frank would later tell me that I needed to defend myself more against COs and stop being afraid to talk back to them. My response was I was trying to get home with no drama whatsoever, not fight every battle. The good thing was these COs didn't mind apologizing. However, because they had so much stress, I never knew when they were cool or when they would snap. I think that's part of the reason it took me so long to loosen up around them.

However, thanks to that grinder and auger being broken in November 2011, I received the most I'd ever made at camp, $83 in a month, which I used to help minimize the need of money from my family. Part of the problem was that trash in the grinder blocked the teeth from grinding the sewage properly, and it suddenly stopped working. So instead of the garbage going into the grinder and up the auger, it sat there blocking the flow. The water and sewage backed up, causing flooding, as much as half a foot of water and sewage. The COs ordered the necessary parts. Due to red tape and politics, the parts for the grinder would take several weeks. Meanwhile, all the powerhouse inmates, with Brasher and Shaw helping us, removed the grinder and adjusted the auger to make it easier to replace the grinder in the future.

Shaw ordered me and my partner to work after hours in the grinding station, in addition to our normal hours, around the last weeks of November 2011. That meant we worked seven days a week: Monday through Friday from 7:00 a.m. to 2:30 p.m. and again for about an hour after 5:00 p.m., then weekends after the 10 a.m. count. The extra hours were to make sure nothing went into the sewer lines.

We went to the grinding station, escorted by the camp CO, and spent about twenty minutes a night doing the station. We had to get the keys from the FCI. I hated looking at the FCI building at night, because it looked like a concrete hell.

While I was working on the grinder, the more tired I was and the less that I worked on my real career. I decided to quit. On my last day, Frank and I went to the grinding station at night. Soon, he talked to the COs about ending the night shift, which they did. Of course, that's after they repaired the grinding machine and augur.

The reason I quit the powerhouse in December 2011 was that I wasn't improving myself. I had a talk with Shaw one day when he pulled me away to teach me a new task. He asked me, "You have a degree, Dandridge. Is this what you really want to do?"

"I just don't want to have to keep going back to dead-end jobs and not go anywhere. I want my books and career to get off and running. But I need something between now and then."

"What do you want out of life, Dandridge?"

"I just don't want to worry about money anymore. I want financial independence."

He shook his head. "Naw, that's not a good answer. You'll lose money in a heartbeat then you'll be unhappy again. Or you'll have money and no happiness. I'm not going to answer that question for you. You got two weeks to figure it out. But think about the other things we've talked about."

We talked about me using my degree to write about my experience in camp to help other people. We talked about me speaking to the public and other groups to educate people on prison life. Shaw and Brasher even talked about me doing something to help change the effects of prison on the individuals and the communities.

In order to quit, I needed to fill out a cop-out, which was a form sent to the admins if an inmate wants to request something from them. I needed to have it signed by the powerhouse COs and the CO from my new job. I already had the first signature from the food service CO. Before Shaw signed the cop-out, Brasher asked me, "So what are you going to do, Dandridge?"

"Follow your advice. I'm going to start by finishing my novel then figure out how to write about this place." I then assured them that I'd respect their privacy and change their names and keep them out the book.

When I was officially out of the powerhouse midway

through December 2011, I was quite happy. I could finally focus on my passions. Don't get me wrong, the powerhouse was good to me, because it kept me busy and I learned a lot. However, it wasn't what I wanted to do long-term.

Frank thought I had given up on my accomplishments at the powerhouse. Though I told him how I felt and what I was going to do, and the COs from the power house recommended I leave, he felt that I had failed him and myself. But I got the impression he still respected me. However, Frank was always willing to take some of the free food that I'd bring back to the dorm or any other hookups I'd offer him.

A few weeks after I left the powerhouse, I found out that due to budget cuts and other prison politics, no one was going to get a certificate of any kind from the powerhouse. Without that certificate, I couldn't show proof that I had HVAC knowledge and I would have had to start from scratch after I got home. It also meant that if I had continued to work at the powerhouse, I would have just wasted time and reduced my chances of turning my true passions into a business. This was especially true considering I was only writing a few minutes a day and as much as possible on the weekends.

Community Service Project

A t first I thought the idea of going home on a fur-lough was unlikely because my sentence was too short. I was also told that I couldn't have a community service project unless I had been there for six months and had at least a year left on my sentence. Though I was disappointed, I just took it as a blessing to get my work done. However, when the second case manager took over, she wanted me to do community service so I could get additional halfway house time. However, because there wasn't any room available to give me additional halfway house time, she decided to give me a five-day furlough.

I was sold on doing the community project. I started the community service project right before Christmas, just days after I quit the powerhouse.

I and four other inmates would start every weekday off by getting a ride from the driver to the FCI. There the COs would take our IDs and verify that we had clearance to leave the camp. Once the CO was finished with us, we would wait in the FCI's visitors' waiting room until our ride to the community project arrived.

The first guy that picked us up was Brian, who was the superintendent. At other times it was Jesse, an elderly man, who got us. Our project was to help Herlong High School redo the floors on the gym. Their gym was smaller than our dorm.

We removed the black smudges from the floors, swept, and then mopped. While other inmates finished stripping and waxing and coating the floor, I and another two inmates fixed the roof on the greenhouse outside. Thankfully, we didn't have any chains or shackles.

At the end of every day, we would return to the FCI, where we were patted down then breath-tested for alcohol. When the COs finished their jobs, we got our IDs back and went back to camp. They also wanted us to be strip-searched after every return to the camp. Thankfully, they never did it.

Helping the school made me feel a little good. Though I liked the people we worked with and the work was easy, I just didn't think it was worth my time.

Again, the whole purpose for me doing community service was to get a five-day furlough or more halfway house time. I wanted to get an extra ninety days at the halfway house, giving me a total of six months, but the new case manager said that I couldn't get more. I figured then that I would do community service for the five-day furlough, thinking that it would help me to get a job and some things lined up at the halfway house. Before I could apply, the rule changed so that we could only get a three-day furlough. There was also the existing rule that we had to pay for transportation to and from, and we had to have a parole officer check out the place where we'd be staying. I told the case manager that it was not worth it. At the time of my decision, I had less than six months before my release. It wasn't worth the money and time.

It was during the community service project that I got to know Yawn Man. He was half Black and half White, and he made his money by trading crochet hats, scarves, and dolls for commissary items. He also was a little eccentric and loopy at times, and really didn't get along with most of the races. However, we appreciated each other's hard work and grew to respect each other. As my sentence was ending, I'd have regular conversations with him about religion and post-prison life. I lost contact with him once I left the camp.

There were other inmates I knew at the camp, but I got closer to them during that community project because I was honest about my intention for doing the community project and because I worked hard even though I didn't like being there. That was in contrast to the Pouch, who complained constantly about the workload. He had a hard time with being in the camp and only did the community project to get out of the camp for as long as he could. He also felt he deserved as much furlough and halfway house time because he worked about nine community service projects, so he told me.

The community service work didn't make me feel better. In fact, once I realized taking a furlough wasn't worth my time, I felt the community service work was pointless. It interfered with my writing, sleep, and work-out time. On one hand, it was nice that the school got some much-needed work done. On the other hand, I hated feeling like free labor. It was bad enough I worked for $80 a month on a good month, but to do the same amount of hours for literally nothing was depressing to me. I wanted to quit, but I was told by the case manager that quitting wasn't allowed.

The next time the secretary and case manager asked me to do another community service opportunity, I said, "No."

"How come?" The secretary gave me a dirty look.

"Because I don't have any incentives," I said with a straight face.

"I'm sorry," Ms. Flores, the case manager said, cutting her eyes at me. "How much longer do you have left?"

"A few weeks," I said.

"We'll see about that," Ms. Flores said, as she allowed me to leave her office.

Luckily for me, nothing came from that conversation. I also never worked another community service event for the camp.

Food Service Job

I started working at the food service line during my community service project midway through December 2011. Working at the food service line instead of the powerhouse was perfect for me. I made $10 a month, which was dramatically less than I was getting at the powerhouse, but my shift was Monday through Friday from 3 p.m. to 5 p.m. When I clocked in at 3 p.m., I'd set up the food items by taking them out of the heating ovens and putting them on the serving line. From there, I'd set up the utensils and wait for 3:30 p.m. Once it came, I, with two or three other inmates, would serve food to all of the food service workers. That line was called short line, because it had the shortest line of inmates coming in. Short line finished at about 3:45 p.m. I would help clean up then sit in the cafeteria until the CO did the out count for food service workers. While he was doing the count, we would play cards until about 4:30 p.m. when the main line was served. I'd serve the inmates just like I did at short line. That line also lasted fifteen minutes, even with giving the inmates seconds. After that it was a quick mop, the food was put back in the hot box, and I was back in the library no later than 5 p.m.

The extra time allowed me to focus on my post-prison

life and to work out more. Plus with all the free food I was allowed to eat and occasionally bring back to my dorm, I stopped buying snacks from commissary and bought shaving cream and deodorant.

Deeply Personal Conversations

I avoided deeply depressing conversations in prison as much as possible.

One time someone told me about their battle with cancer. Someone else told me that his wife had brain cancer. A third inmate told me he was having trouble with his children acting up. When I was on the freeway, I sat in my bunk one day and was extremely depressed because I was dying of cancer, my wife had brain cancer, and I didn't know what to do with my kids. I had to remember that I didn't even have kids or a wife. I didn't have cancer. That's when I realized that I internalized everyone's problems. I remember being depressed about that for most of the day.

A few new people would be very talkative and clingy. Maybe it was their way of coping with a new experience or their idea of home was to be included and connected with other inmates. I just wasn't going to allow people to cling to me.

My way of coping was to stay away from others and watch from a distance while analyzing my thoughts, observations, and emotions. Sure, I whined and questioned as much as anyone. However, I minimized it by accepting the fact I was there and I was almost done. My way of coping was to find the positives in camp and focus on the brighter future. I also wanted to focus on making this the best damn experience in the world. It worked out to be a type of coping. If clinging was what some people needed, I could respect that. However, I think people learned quickly who they could be clingy to and who they should avoid. They would figure everything out in the coming months.

Once inmates started talking about their problems, if I couldn't give them a solution, I avoided the conversation or changed the subject. I couldn't deal with them bringing me down because they were lonely, depressed, or horny.

I think that's how I got a reputation for being too immature to have deep conversations. I took it and rolled with it and thought that wasn't true. However, the end result meant that I didn't have those conversations.

Inmate Whining

There's a lot of complaining at camp. I heard inmates complain they didn't want to be there, they shouldn't be there, they're bored, tired, lonely, horny, or whatever. Most inmates from higher institutions said, "Don't bring your ass to prison next time," or "Yeah, you wanna sell drugs and rob people, and you wanna complain about getting caught and going to jail? You knew what you got yourself into."

From what I understood from the inmates at higher institutions, camp was either very boring because there weren't a lot of things to do, or it was the most freedom they had in years. The COs were not as strict, the rules were more flexible, and they didn't have to watch their backs every second. One inmate, who worked his way down from a low-security institution, said, "Camp is sweet. I'm trying to stay here as long as possible."

However, inmates who self-surrendered felt like camp was hell and prison combined. They felt they should have the same rights as they had before prison camp—rights such as sleeping in their own beds, seeing their loved ones as much as they wanted, or being able to move around whenever they wanted. Some of these inmates felt they didn't deserve to be there or they should be treated like inmates in Europe, who go home to their families on weekends. Some of these inmates were drug offenders and some were white-collar criminals. Some of the drug offenders had been in state, local, or federal prison before, while there were others who were first-time offenders. Most of the white-collar criminals at the camp when I was there were first-time offenders.

It seemed, however, the white-collar criminals had the hardest adjustment curve out of all the inmates I've seen. These inmates had shorter sentences, usually less than three years, and used to have great jobs and a comfortable suburban lifestyle. They seemed to be the type of people who got what they wanted by asking for it or working for it. When they came to prison camp, that became less true because those comforts and lifestyles were for law-abiding citizens. As inmates, they were treated the same way as all the other camp inmates were by the COs. In fact, some COs were from higher-security prisons and couldn't treat camp inmates the same as other inmates.

Because of that, COs and inmates from higher-security prisons would look at these white-collar criminals as whiny, ungrateful, and entitled. I heard often that those white-collar criminals couldn't survive in high-security prisons because they couldn't even handle the ebbs and flows of the camp. White-collar criminals seemed to want to complain to anyone who would listen to them, and they would repeatedly complain about the same issues.

Those inmates gave the impression that they were better than the other inmates by saying, "I'm too good to be at a camp" or "My crime wasn't as bad as a drug dealer so why am I here? I shouldn't be around these people." These statements were interpreted to mean that they were superior to higher-security inmates. However, when an inmate from a higher-security institution confronted those white-collar inmates, the white-collars would backpedal, retracting their statements with an apology or saying, "I was just joking, man, don't take it so personal." A lot of inmates from the higher-security institutions would avoid white-collars for that reason alone. However, depending on the white-collar's race, inmates of that race might try to keep him close and mentor him for prison camp life.

White-collars were not the only ones complaining and whining. Inmates would complain because the policy would not always properly enforced. Policy is the term used for the rules and regulations listed in the Inmate Handbook. This handbook has rules set by the Department of Justice and Herlong Prison Camp. The handbook lists the behavior expected from inmates and COs. It also has the possible punishments for inmates and COs. To my knowledge, COs could get the same punishment as inmates if they violated policy. In addition to the handbook, there was documents on the TRULINCS system with additional memos and documents of rules and procedures. Also, there were additional policy memos and documents posted along the walls of the dorm.

At times, the policies would also be misunderstood by the COs and admins who enforced them. Other times COs would be flexible with prison camp policies by allowing inmates to get away with things that normally would merit disciplinary actions. Sometimes it was having weights, or bringing food back to the dorm, or walking around the camp without the required black boots during business hours. Yet when a CO came in and enforced the correct policy, such as black boots during business hours, inmates would get upset and feel as if they were being told too many different things at once. Because inmates got comfortable with the slack enforcement or didn't know the policy, they would feel as if the camp admins were picking on them or the admins were playing politics at their expenses. Sometimes that would be true. However, in the case of the black shoes, that policy was in the handbook and should have been enforced.

Inmates, COs, and admins thought they were going according to policy, which was treated like it was the Bible or Constitution. It was difficult for me to understand the policy. At times it changed at random, and I usually referred to the inmates I trusted to help interpret the policy for me. It was those inmates who told me when the COs would go along with policy and when they would go against it, and how to act accordingly.

As much as we hated it, we just had to deal with the inconsistency of the policy enforcement and take it as just the ebb and flow of the camp. I only had a year or so, no need to get upset over those issues. These problems didn't bother inmates from higher-security prisons because it was still less drama than what they dealt with at other prisons. They didn't have to watch their backs, deal with politics, or work around ten-minute moves.

They also thought that the COs were pretty chill compared to the ones they had dealt with behind the wall.

Frank told me one day that he never got comfortable at camp. He was afraid that if he did, he would not appreciate how good camp life was, and he wanted to be ready to be moved to a low-security prison, which in his opinion could have happened at any time. I noticed that inmates from a higher-security prison who got used to camp life started having similar entitlements and complaints as the white-collars.

Another thing I witnessed were inmates, regardless of the type of inmate, who were upset with the admins because they didn't get what they wanted, and who complained and whined about the same points over and over. Then they would agree with someone telling them that they were wrong, and then they would disagree with a statement whether it contradicted everything they said, actually agreed with the point, or rambled off-subject.

There was one dude who wanted more halfway house time because people coming after him got more halfway house time (six months) but did nothing to earn it, while he had to do community service just to get four months on a twenty-seven-month sentence. The minimum amount of halfway house time awarded was normally 10 percent of the inmates' sentence, which in his case would have been two months. He should have gotten three months and two five-day furloughs.

A furlough is when the warden grants an inmate time away from the camp. Furloughs allow the inmate to reestablish ties in the community, look for jobs, or to get housing ready for release. In order for the inmate to go home on a furlough, he had to meet the requirements set by the case manager.

Here's the funny thing about a furlough. Most inmates would get either a one- to three-day furlough or an extra thirty days of halfway house time. Many inmates mistakenly claimed that the one- to three-day furloughs had the same value as thirty days in a halfway house. I understand that it's not a one-to-one equivalent. However, most of the time, if an inmate got a furlough, he didn't get the additional halfway house time, and vice versa.

When I was working in the kitchen, an overweight inmate named Tiny got upset at me because I wouldn't give him extra food. The COs and cooks said one scoop for seconds, and so I did as told. He got pissed at me again, so the CO cussed him out and gave him two scoops. He didn't talk to me anymore and stared me down a few times from the food line and in the dorm. I ignored him because I didn't want to get in trouble over trivial stuff.

The camp had been silly at times. In the weeks near the end of my sentence, the camp was changing. People weren't courteous like they were when I first got there. People grouped together in the aisle, talking and sitting and blocking the way, not moving for people who were walking by. The inmate back talk got more personal, with people not respecting each other's feelings.

I saw more selfish behavior and people trying to push buttons and boundaries. The camp was losing inmate leadership, and the inmates were becoming too individualistic with too many out for themselves and not caring about other inmates. There were too many people proving their worth to themselves at the expense of others with no consideration for other people and their feelings.

I think the problem was that most people only responded to confrontation, meaning that people felt their world was fine until there was a confrontation or immediate danger. They went about their selfish ways until the CO or the administration boss came down on the inmate or the CO. From there, shit rolled downhill. If they get cussed out, we got it worse.

It all felt like things could explode at any moment, which would only further hurt the inmates in the future. However, no one would care until they got caught in the crossfire, and those who were smooth enough would find their way out of it while others would get busted and complain that they didn't have anything and that no one cared about them.

A week before I left the camp, we had a town hall meeting in the dorm ran by the camp counselor with the assistant warden and a few other COs and lieutenants from the FCI. It was less of a meeting and more a reminder of the rules that we were supposed to obey such as not having food service food in our lockers, not having chairs in the aisles, not blocking high-traffic areas, and keeping everything clean. Also, the orderlies had to get rid of any extra chairs in the dorm. There was supposed to be one chair per inmate. Somehow, there were several chairs. In fact, I had one chair in my square and one in the television room. Rumor had it that some people from the Department of Justice were coming to inspect the camp so they wanted everything to be perfect. No more food or any kitchen-related items, which we shouldn't have in the dorms anyway. Also, we couldn't have commissary food in the kitchen area. Now there are policies, but they're not going to be enforced. And why the town hall meeting?

I had no idea why the acting assistant warden was there, but he threatened to lock down the camp. After saying, "I'm here for the week," he immediately left the town hall meeting.

When the inmates had a chance to ask questions, instead of asking important questions about fairness from the COs and admins, they asked about getting more furloughs, better food, and visiting procedures, which did little for the overall well-being of the inmates. One inmate even asked about having to wear his black boots all day to and from work, a question that had been answered thousands of times by the admins. These questions were answered dismissively by the administrators. The meeting ended with a warning that we needed to police ourselves and keep ourselves accountable for our actions. However, if we had a problem we were to contact the CO or the administration for assistance. Most inmates tuned the meeting out. In fact, the inmates from higher-security institutions didn't even pay attention to the whole meeting.

I actually thought the meeting was a sign that things were going to get tough at the camp. However, the rules continued to get broken. The chairs, for example, continued to be used and left by inmates until we had a shakedown. We waited until shift change and went back to business as usual. We became cautious about the days and times when we did what we did. It was the same with the chairs.

The Silliness of Herlong Camp

One night, Pulitzer and Kells were having a shouting match over who could use a certain shower stall. Pulitzer had his clothes on the stall door, but Kells decided to use it because Pulitzer was talking too long to use that shower. By the time Pulitzer was ready to shower, Kells was already there, completely naked and covered in soap. Pulitzer told Kells to get out of the shower immediately.

The result was a huge screaming match with Pulitzer shouting, "I don't care. Tell the fucking CO. Don't touch my shit." He really didn't care because Kells was fully naked in the shower. Kells was afraid and sounded as if he was going to cry but finished his shower.

The other campers made fun of both old men. Luckily no one got in trouble mainly because the CO was walking around outside the dorms. The funny thing was, most of the shower stalls were available. That particular one wasn't the best stall because it was in front and in view of inmates in high-traffic areas.

One day, Bigboy got fired from the kitchen for eating unauthorized food, which usually meant stolen eggs. However, inmates questioned the firing because the eggs were locked away and were usually given to the inmates under supervision of the food service CO.

Inmates never touched the COs keys, even if they hit the ground in front of them. I understood that even during the cooking process, inmates were watched and the ingredients were accounted for by the food service CO. The mere fact that the inmate touched them would be considered stealing, I was told. It didn't make sense to most of the camp inmates that Bigboy would get in trouble for this. The camp CO in the dorm busted him and not the food service CO. Many camp inmates believed Bigboy was set up so the dorm CO didn't get in trouble. However, there was very little proof to prove a CO did take the eggs.

Maybe that inmate should have known, but it really seemed like a setup. That's the kind of crap that goes on here. However, Bigboy was one of the only inmates who didn't have a job because he got fired from every job for stealing or not working.

Another day, an inmate, who was one of the best bakers in the camp, finally went home after a fifteen-year sentence. He left his locker cluttered and dirty. It was full of garbage and old food. We all laughed but sympathized with his pissed bunky because that was cold-blooded and rude. However, what could anyone do but laugh or help? I took him two garbage cans to clear out dirty underwear, garbage, and old food.

One day we had a softball game. The final score was 26–24, thanks to no one playing defense because the sun was in everyone's eye. They pitched underhanded and had Frank and Blue as the umpires. The winners got powdered drink mixes from the recreation department.

The game was fun to watch. During the game, people were talking shit. After an inmate kept hollering "weak spot," he got into it with Fake Pastor. The inmate, who was smoking in the stands, was actually talking about the inmate in center field. However, Fake Pastor took it personally and the two argued and bickered the three innings that I was there. They also bickered through the following week. Strangely enough, it was actually funny listening to everyone assuming the other team was cheating and questioning the umpires.

Snitches in Control

The snitches were strong in Herlong Camp when I was there. I saw a lot of white-collar criminals walk around bragging about being a snitch. It was as if it gave them power or some kind of authority over other inmates who transferred from the higher-security prisons.

As long as I was there, I never saw a snitch get beaten or physically hurt. Mostly, I've seen most inmates avoiding snitches at all costs. Many inmates believed a snitch would turn on an inmate at a drop of a hat just for the respect of the COs and admins.

About three months into my sentence, an inmate went to the hole for having an MP3 player, which was considered as bad as having a cell phone, and came back within two weeks. It usually took three weeks for an inmate to get a hearing for his case. Meanwhile, most inmates would have to stay in the SHU until proven innocent. How did this inmate get out in less than two weeks, if it's true that it took three to four weeks just for a hearing? Most inmates assumed he snitched on someone so he wasn't trusted.

One inmate, Baseball, was always in the leisure library with me. He loved baseball and the Bible. They were the only things that he talked about, except his friendships with the warden and the camp administrators. He was an orderly for the FCI's guest room and visiting room. Whenever Baseball heard someone complaining, he'd say, "Yeah, I'm going to talk to the warden on Monday. He'll always listen to me." He would continuously talk as if the two of them had lunch and coffee after work. I just thought to myself, "If the warden ever cared about the camp, a lot of inmates would be in a lot of trouble or be moved to a low-security prison."

Baseball was just one of several inmates who bragged about knowing the admins and warden. Rumor had it that these snitches would get some minor luxuries like easier jobs or advance notice on fire drills or raids in exchange for being the eyes and ears of the camp.

I think the COs and admins chronically lied to the inmates. They would tell us what we wanted to hear or what they knew we could spread around the camp. For example, an inmate told me that they were going to start reducing our sentences because of overcrowding. He claimed to get the information from the camp counselor. But there were no reduced sentences for inmates due to overcrowding. There was another rumor that inmates would be allowed to take longer furloughs if they completed certain tasks. That ended up not being true also.

In fact, we all had to be careful because some of those inmates were really undercover police officers or COs. It was believed that GM6 had a major shakedown because a police officer posing as an inmate told the GM6 COs about the wrongdoings of the inmates. The result was that five inmates got fired from the assignment.

That's why inmates avoided talking about sensitive

information around inmates they didn't trust. Snitches were always looking for some dirt on other inmates to use as blackmail. Therefore, they ear hustled (eavesdropped on) as many conversations as possible.

According to what the inmates told me, snitches were the cheapest way to govern and regulate the system. They were very quick to tell on a person, mainly because they couldn't fight. I talked to two snitches who told me to my face that they had no problem snitching. It's the passive evil way of getting back at bullying. I didn't argue with it.

One inmate, Danny the Jew, admitted to me that he'd snitched on inmates and had fake cell phones just in case anyone picked on him or gave him problems. He told me that it gave him power over other inmates who could fight better than him. If an inmate ever gave him a problem, he could just put a cell phone on him. If the inmate got caught, he would get a 100-series shot (which added points to an inmate's record and could make him lose camp status), a $75 fine, and about six months in the hole. The inmate would most likely be moved to another camp or prison. I kept my distance from him, though we did get along very well.

However, snitching only made inmates look like bitches to other inmates and the authorities. The CO didn't respect a snitch because he saw him as someone who couldn't fight for himself or who didn't have problem-solving skills. Shaw told me several stories about how he hated inmates snitching on other inmates. He didn't respect those snitches because they were snitching on the same people who were protecting and taking care of them. He told me that some snitches were desperate for rewards and thought snitching was the way to get it. Of course, if the snitch told Shaw something, he had to look into it. Regardless of the outcome, Shaw, like most COs, wouldn't trust or respect the snitch afterward. Shaw also said, "If a snitch can do that to an inmate, he'd snitch on me too."

Sex in Prison Camp

Let me just say, I never saw any homosexual acts in prison camp. I never saw anyone having sex with COs or other visitors at Herlong.

That's not saying that it never happened, I just never saw it. I did see a lot of pictures of women in bikinis. I saw that a lot of inmates watched those housewife shows and sexy music videos.

At first I was trying to stop all masturbation and sexual thoughts. I thought I would get sent to the hole if I did anything. Plus I felt strange being around a bunch of men thinking and talking about sex. So I tried to suppress it.

But what I suppressed came back stronger. I fantasized about woman I wished I'd been with, and others that I had been with and missed. I normally listened to meditation CDs when I wrote or read, and it was getting difficult at times to focus on that.

So I wrote about my needs and wants in my journal. It was not as good as the real thing, but it allowed me to get it all off my chest. The writing minimized my need for sex. Any other need that I had, I took care of in the shower, alone.

Other inmates discussed their past sexual exploits or handled their business in the shower. There were rumors, such as prostitutes in the library and inmates having sex with COs, but there was no evidence that I could see.

Once I found myself writing about it, in a letter or a journal, it allowed me to focus on writing this book as well as other projects. That method was very helpful. There also weren't a lot of options for me to do anything. It was either the shower or bathroom. I have to say that neither was very pleasant.

My other issue with sex was the fact that I wished I could have been with more women than I had been. There was a regret I had that was similar to what I felt about living the life that I wanted to live. I had been with women that I hadn't been happy with. I was with women for one thing and women who only wanted me for one thing. I even let a few good ones slide away only to realize later that I wished I had them right now, not to mention the women I couldn't date because I was going to prison camp. Maybe I missed having the option to turn women down.

There in prison camp, there was no access to women that I could see. Maybe I just didn't look for the opportunities. As I keep saying, all I wanted to do was get home with some sanity left. I wasn't going to allow a need for sex to get in my way. I lost my virginity at twenty-five because I wanted to understand myself better and prevent the sins of my father. There were also several periods of my life when I didn't have sex for years, like when I was taking a break from dating or because the options weren't there. Therefore, I wasn't going to let a year without sex be an issue to me.

I didn't even see those female COs as women. Okay, I have to admit some did look pretty nice, but not nice enough to risk extending my sentence.

My New Bunky

My bunky YT got sent to the hole after a CO believed he had "something" suspicious in his hand and was out of bounds.

That was the first time since I was on the freeway that I had the whole bunk to myself. The first thing I did was to put some of his stuff in my locker to hide it from the other inmates. He had a lot of books about yoga and metaphysics. I figured I'd find some way of mailing them to his home if anything happened. I then spent the day writing on the desk at my bunk space. I didn't like writing at my bunk because people kept talking to me about what happened to my bunky.

Most of that night, the CO went through YT's locker to pack up his belongings. He was slamming doors and asking me questions about YT's stuff. He offered me detergent and deodorant as well as food that he didn't want to pack. I took it in the hope of being able to give it back to YT. The CO started at 2:30 a.m. on a Sunday morning and didn't stop until 3:45 a.m. That morning, I got of bed at 8:19 a.m.

I put in a request to get the bottom bunk. I just wanted to avoid getting a joker or a loser as a bunky and to maintain the necessary respect in the cube. However, the camp counselor merely said, "I'll consider it." Other inmates told me he wouldn't give me the bottom bunk because I had so little time left.

Within the week, my new bunky moved in. NB was a middle-aged man from Jamaica. I think I drove him crazy because I was so focused on getting my books done that I really didn't trip on the politics of the camp. Luckily, the politics in the camp were very minimal so that wasn't a real issue. I also think that I was a bit too cocky and sensitive to his dry humor. I took several of his jokes personally until I knew him better and I just assumed everything he said was a joke.

NB was in camp for knowing someone who was convicted of a crime, as it was told to me. I admit I could be wrong, but he didn't tell on the person and was accused of being an accomplice. I'm sure by now he's home safe with his loved ones.

Once we got past our differences in humor and taste, we actually were great friends.

He gave me some insights about how to really act in prison camp because he was from a low-security prison. I saw him as an older brother. I did have a "younger brother" mentality about me which seemed to work well when getting along with other inmates.

I think he liked me because if I had extra, he had extra. That's how that works. I made sure he was cool just like I did my last bunky, YT. I didn't like being in the bunk all day. I really was at the bunk for count and sleeping, nothing else. My NB got to sleep in, take naps, or whatever he wanted to do, as long as he didn't mess with my stuff. Of course, that wasn't an issue anyway.

Yoga Racial Tension

YT returned from the hole a month later because the arresting CO couldn't prove YT was holding an object or even identify what the object was. They released him after giving him a 300 series shot for being out of bounds and revoking his commissary and phone privileges for a month. It was the best possible outcome for him.

The Black inmates tried to keep YT's slot for yoga open by holding workout sessions during his assigned time in the room because they had so much drama getting it before I arrived. If an inmate wasn't there to host his class, other inmates would try to use the room regardless of the posted times. The Blacks didn't do a good job of holding the room because they had other obligations during that time, and a group of White inmates tried to take the room for their workouts. Those White inmates tried to make it sound as if we only wanted the room for Blacks only. They suggested that we share the room with other races. However, those same inmates didn't allow other inmates to join their workouts unless they were part of their circle, which was a common practice among inmates.

Only three Blacks had joined the yoga class. However,

he was one of our own and we weren't going to allow someone to interfere with his development or progress.

It was just me and YT during his first class after coming back from the hole. The other nine-to-twelve inmates who wanted to use the room were Mexican, White, and Asian.

Well, the White boys didn't want to get out of the room. They threatened to fight us if we didn't leave, so we got the brothers—four White dudes versus ten brothers in the room. Suddenly, the White dudes claimed that they never threatened to fight us, and they calmed down.

But YT gave them the room because the non-Black inmates were afraid of retaliation from those White inmates. YT didn't want to get in that kind of trouble, and physical violence would get all of us in the hole and shipped out. So he backed down. Our class was running out of time anyway. Yet the Blacks warned him only to call them when he really wanted to throw down.

On the next scheduled yoga date, class was again canceled because of the same drama. The Whites wanted to split the room and work out on one side while we practiced yoga and meditated on the other. We turned down the deal because it was hard to split the room and do yoga and meditation because the Whites played loud heavy metal music and grunted during their workout sessions. We ended up agreeing on Monday, Thursday, and Friday for yoga.

I really enjoyed my yoga classes, so it was very annoying when I couldn't practice yoga because of that drama. We had an agreement, it was set, but now we had to deal with garbage all the time. We agreed on Sunday, Wednesday, and Friday. If those inmates didn't work out, we would practice yoga.

It turned out that four of those inmates were sent to the hole because they had supposedly made threats to a CO for not forcing a middle-aged inmate with hepatitis to quit. When they didn't get their way, they made life hard for the inmate by putting ice in his bed and harassing him in his sleep.

Because of that event, we got an extra day, Monday. By the time of my release, the class had grown to fourteen students and YT added a metaphysical class.

Homesickness and Loneliness

I often felt alone and disconnected from everyone. When I first arrived at camp, I stayed to myself to focus on my writing and because I didn't know anyone there well enough to open up to them. I'd developed an antisocial attitude in general—but I wasn't a snob. Mainly I felt I didn't always fit in with the other inmates. The Blacks talked loud, and I was quiet. I wanted to focus on my future career because I wanted to see that camp experience as a perfect opportunity to get my life right. In doing so, I created a massive distance between me and other inmates. When I did that, however, I felt cut off from the general public.

I understood the difficulty of that situation. It was painful because I didn't have the choice to spend the time I wanted to with my friends and family. That choice was made for me, and I was the only person to blame for it. I couldn't help but to think of hugging and kissing and laughing with everyone at home. Not to mention, I regretted not spending more time with them. I continuously had regrets about not spending enough time with family members and friends. I regretted spending more time working at a job than I did interacting with the people I had things in common with.

I started thinking, what would have happened if I

didn't catch a case? I'd be out of state or just transferring back to Sacramento, maybe. I would have lost connection with everyone but would have had a grand party when I saw them.

The connection to the real world and my real world was what I'd missed the most. I had missed my friends mainly because they were real, and their voices and letters and emails reminded me of something real.

Don't get me wrong, I believe those inmates were good men and they treated me very well. However, I knew they wouldn't last very long in my life, so I couldn't have the same emotional investment in them as I would in my friends at home.

Some inmates were loyal to their race and groups. Even with that type of inmate, I knew not to get too attached because they could be at camp one day and shipped off the next day. And other inmates were just friends to people to get anything they could out of them. Those type of inmates were referred to as opportunists.

Other inmates didn't want to be bothered because they felt their time would go by smoother if they reduced the number of friends that they had. The women were fake and in the form of pictures, television, memories, and stories, none of which could be touched.

In addition, the friends that I made there weren't lifelong friends. They came and went. Suddenly they would all be in the solitary housing unit, transferred or released. I questioned whether inmates had friends to make them better as a man, as I would do with them, or whether they made friends to pass the time.

Back at home, I rarely spent time with friends or

networked with other people because I worked mainly nights at a local restaurant. I might send a series of texts or a have a quick five-minute conversation or talk to them on social media.

However, when I went into camp, I lost the ability to contact them at my leisure or on social media. The telephone, TRULINCS, and mailing letters were the only ways I could talk to them. Most of my friends didn't feel comfortable talking to me over the phone because it was recorded, and they didn't know if the government was keeping their numbers on file. Other friends and family didn't answer unknown or blocked calls, and when I called them, the caller ID would say either "blocked" or "unknown." Some of my family had collection calls, and I didn't want to take the chance of having to talk to them. They also had their own moral reasons for not wanting to talk to me while in camp. Even when I did get to talk to my friends and family, the phone would disconnect the call at exactly fifteen minutes, with warning about a minute before disconnecting. The TRULINCS system was difficult for some of my friends to understand, while others didn't feel comfortable giving the government their email addresses. And most of my friends and family didn't have time around their busy schedule to write letters.

The homesick feeling was real bad one day. We watched *Tron: Legacy* for our weekend institution movie during my first weekend at camp. It was the second time I'd watched it. The first time I watched it with my cousin in a movie theater. Usually when I watched movies, it was over at his house or other family members' homes. But while I was watching this movie at camp, I felt like I was at home, watching a movie with my cousin. After the movie ended, I realized that I was in prison and became depressed. It was more of a feeling of being homesick. I would have that problem a few times during the first few weeks. After that, it was normal.

Luckily I wasn't in camp during Mother's Day, but Father's Day was painful because I only talked to my stepfather for a few minutes. Our family didn't celebrate those holidays, but those days were reminders that I was removed from my parents and yet another reminder that I was in prison camp. Normally I would just tell them Happy Father's Day or Mother's Day and we would go about our day. Yet on that Father's Day, I didn't spend any time with him and I couldn't see him during visiting hours because of his job's restrictions. It felt like yet another person who was removed because of my mistake and my camp situation. He was someone I talked to regularly, and I was living with him before I went to camp. For me to only talk to him sparingly made that day even more painful.

It really made me think about my past relationships and how I didn't spend the time I wanted to with the people I should have.

Another difficult moment was when my cousins' father passed and I couldn't do anything to support them. They didn't ask me to, but they wouldn't have had to anyway. What bugged me was that I'm usually there when times were hard, but not that time. All I could do was offer my condolences and remove it from my memory to avoid letting it eat me up inside.

Luckily, I had my mom really keep an eye on the people that I'd worried about. I also knew that my family would rally around those who really needed the help.

So I guess I had it lucky, because some cats here were continuously depressed over the fact they couldn't help with simple or complex household responsibilities because we'd been shipped over here as a form of correction or rehabilitation. Yet the family structure was one of the greatest forms of rehabilitation.

The holidays added to my loneliness. Instead of eating with family and having my grandma's amazing soul food, I had camp Thanksgiving food. The food was edible, and the most food that we would have at one time during my stay there. We had turkey, ham, cranberry sauce, mashed potatoes, and other sides. I saved the meat for dinner. I didn't like the stuffing which had cranberries, celery, carrots, onions, and breading. The salad was very bland. We also got a free Coke, which I gave away. Technically, that Thanksgiving dinner was a lunch, because it was served at 10:30 a.m. We got a sack with four pieces of bread, bologna meat, peanut butter cookies, and mini pretzels for dinner. It was a far cry from the turkey, ham, mac and cheese, oysters, yams, greens, and nine different types of pies I would have at my grandma's house. What made that so bad was that it was my favorite holiday because that was when all the family would go to my grandmother's house. The family would miss Christmas, most of the birthdays, and other family outings. But it seemed like no matter what, they made Thanksgiving, come hell or high water.

My birthday was strange because I felt so disconnected and depressed. However, I didn't celebrate my birthday that often. I figured it was no big deal. No, it was one of the most depressing days of camp. Once I got through my birthday, camp was much more manageable.

Getting letters from home and connecting with real people from my home was a big help. One way to cure my loneliness was to start writing letters to friends. I had a few pen pals I wrote to and a good list of friends on my email list.

I kept in contact with as many family members as I could by email and by phone. I emailed my core and intimate relatives weekly. My mom sent me magazines from the *Sacramento Business Journal* every month as well as other magazines about how to set up my website after I got home.

My mom also started typing my novel *Crime and Punishment* and helped with getting my driver's license and diploma. She also kept my spirits high and gave me encouragement.

I still have a mass email from all the family that I received for Christmas. My aunt and uncle sent me money for my birthday.

When my mom visited, she updated me on all the family business and gossip. It was funny though, she rarely mentioned anything negative about the family. Maybe it was because she knew that I would internalize it, or maybe because I had it harder than any other family member and she assumed I didn't want to hear a bunch of whining. I could see any of those points.

Mail, email and snail mail, did not come very often. During the week, I could go by without hearing from the family and friends, but weekends were a little difficult. I made one phone call at least.

As far as the need for other inmates to protect me from physical violence, it was needed and necessary to get through the pettiness of the camp. Inmates from high-security prisons told me there was less need for protection compared to other prisons. However, I noticed that if people knew I associated with inmates like Frank regularly, they were less likely to deal with me, mainly because they didn't want to deal with Frank, or any of the other Blacks I associated with regularly. Though camp inmates were not known for fighting, associating with highly respected inmates regularly kept the drama away from me.

I needed counseling and advice, but I couldn't get that from the camp counselor or chaplain. If the counselor had cared about my problems, he would have sent me to the psychologist. The chaplain was also useless as far as showing compassion for an inmate's problems, but he'd listen for a few minutes before sending inmates to the psychologist, and probably pray for them.

Finding Spirituality

O f course, the one advantage of being in prison camp was that I could work on my inner self. I could become more spiritual and less religious. During my time there, I looked into and read about religions such as Wicca, various Islamic branches, Judaism, and Christianity. I found some things that made me appreciate those religions, although I didn't see myself following them.

It was studying Ramtha and learning my chakra system that gave me the greatest peace and brought me to a spiritual closure that I had only imagined. I didn't agree with everything that Ramtha said. However, what I took from the book was using my consciousness and energy to create the reality that I wanted. It strongly stressed that humans and God were one and the same. The book also discussed how removing all self-hate and focusing on giving to another man was the charity that was going to "free" me from this world. He mentioned that people wanted to focus on the void which was "one vast nothing, all things potential." He believed that creation started because of a thought into this void. I took it to mean that I could make anything out of nothing if I really wanted to believe that it was possible.

I was also doing Dahn yoga, which focuses on the

chakras. Chakras, according to yoga philosophy, are any of several points, or wheels, of physical or spiritual energy in the human body. There are six points on a person's body and one over his head. One of these chakras, the Dahn Jahn, which is located two inches below the navel, is considered to be one of the strength energy points in a human. Dahn yoga focuses on breathing and stretching. The instructor told me to do only the poses I could manage. In time, the poses get easier to do. I saw people with bad knees struggle with yoga, but within a few weeks they were able to stretch like they never had a problem. I've learned to let strength in. The philosophies of Ramtha helped me to not only believe in it but fuel energy to it. The class was taught by YT, who was a student of Dahn yoga as well as lessons from Ramtha.

YT also taught the class a technique where I could force energy from my crown to my feet and back and forth. It's called the vibrational state. If I did it for ten minutes, I'd find myself able to refocus. In the morning, I sent the energy up and down my body and then focused on the Dahn Jahn. Then I started writing, and it seemed as if my hands were fueled with that energy.

It was also during that class I learned a forgiveness prayer which was also helpful. After a few deep breaths, I pictured someone I didn't like and repeated that prayer twenty-seven times: "I forgive you, you forgive me, we forgive each other, we forgive ourselves, please divine, thank you, please divine, amen."

I found that I was immediately not angry at these people. It became difficult to think about that person and easier to move forward. I decided to change the word *forgive* to other words and see how they would affect me. The words I found the most helpful were *trust, accept, love,* and *need.*

That same yoga class also taught me about frequency statements. They were much like affirmations in that I told myself what I "am" and spoke in the present tense as if it "is" happening or "always was happening." I didn't find this as successful as the prayer above, however.

The class also taught me that patience was living in a state of no time. That helped me become patient and not rush things or projects or success. Things happened when it was necessary, not necessarily because I caused them to happen.

One of the most powerful spiritually related things that happened to me was a dream I had about a bridge.

It was a long, endless bridge that was surrounded by water and endless skies. The start of the bridge was a bubble which contained all my past thoughts and people I knew. I could see them. However, if I ever went in, I'd see nothing but dusk, gas, and lightning. I would never see those people.

There was a guide. Sometimes he looked half-human, half-lamb. Other times, he looked like me. But he always told me to never think about what I didn't want. I was to only focus on what I wanted to happen. If I had a negative thought while walking on the bridge, dangerous animals like sharks, lions, or even dinosaurs would appear on the bridge, with little or no explanation. However, if I had positive and uplifting thoughts, I would have gentle breezes, sunshine, or even dolphins swimming in the water. Also, the atmosphere would be peaceful and still, and I would be able to walk further down the bridge.

At the beginning of that bridge, I was super self-conscious and nervous about everything. I didn't want to let go of that bubble or to be too far from it. That's when all the crazy animals would appear and earthquakes and tidal waves would happen. As I moved away from the bubble, the more confident I was about walking down the bridge. As a result, fewer things happened. In fact, nothing happened. It was like Sunday strolling on a sunny day. However, at the end, I saw what I thought was a city of gold. There I found a few of my friends from the past and new friends I had never met in real life.

I always thought that the dream was my way of telling myself that I couldn't go back to the way things were. However, if I kept going in this direction, things would actually be better. Those friends would come back if it was God's intention. When I bridged, it was comforting. Regardless of how optimistic I tried to be, I would fear for my future.

Another important aspect of my developing spirituality was writing. Writing in prison was a way to work out my problems. It was like having a counselor who truly understood me without judgment. I could say anything to the paper by way of the pen and no one would know, mainly because my handwriting was sloppy as hell. But I also didn't write anything people cared about reading.

I felt like I could get into myself on so many levels with it. I could put thoughts on paper in ways that I couldn't say out loud.

Religion in Prison

The majority of inmates kept their religion to themselves. I think that this was in part because inmates didn't want to hear other inmates preach a gospel or philosophy that the messenger himself didn't follow. It seemed that the majority of the inmates thought if someone wanted to know something, they would ask.

There were also inmates who would preach to whoever wanted to discuss it. Those same inmates looked down on non-Christian believers. They felt that they were somehow in greater favor with God, or their version of God, because of how they worshiped. I tried to avoid religious debates and conversations whenever possible because they were just too difficult and draining.

The conversations wasn't about expressing their own beliefs and trying to learn from others' beliefs. It was about proving who was right or wrong. These conversations were never fruitful unless the inmate was a Christian pastor or someone inmates considered an authority.

I felt that people could be in prison and convert to Christianity to be a better person. I saw people in prison camp who were using religion for selfish reasons such as to prove that they were programming. Other inmates used it to get instant forgiveness from their wrongdoings.

I also found that some inmates used religion as escapism to get away from the realities of prison camp. However, it's hard for me to say that these people were wrong. I had seen people lose their minds because of depression and anxiety because of the stresses of camp. To my understanding, all the doctors and counselors did was listen and give them a pill. That practice was very ineffective. I've seen inmates walk around like a zombie or sleeping for long hours because of the medication.

If religion gave an inmate any sanity, even if the depictions were inaccurate, I totally understood.

Some inmates used religion to understand the error of their ways and better themselves upon their release. I applauded them for using those teachings to help them move forward in life. These types of inmates would keep their beliefs to themselves, and they avoided talking about them because it was their personal relationship with their god and no one else.

The problem I had was with the people who felt that they had to preach their version of Christ to inmates as if they were high-and-mighty. We ate the same food and lived in the same dorm as everyone else. These high-and-mighty inmates would gossip in the library or in the multipurpose room. These inmates would also be the first inmates to snitch to admins and COs because they believed, or claimed, they were acting under the guidelines of the Bible.

Another problem I had was inmates who knowingly broke the rules, such as stealing, and then told me that "the Bible says thou shall not steal." These inmates would be found with several items that would be considered contraband, and they stole items from kitchen. Most inmates saw these inmates as hypocritical, and were only cordial to them or used them for personal gain.

Camp Lockdowns

Lockdown was when the warden shut down the yard and locked everyone in their cell. It was like the entire prison and camp was in the SHU or hole. All activities would be limited and privileges were mostly revoked or suspended. At the camp, we were only stuck inside the dorm for a few hours. Unlike the camp, the inmates at the FCI would only be allowed to come outside one hour a day, and even then only selected sections at a time would be allowed to use their hour. The inmates at the FCI were not allowed to work at their jobs, eat in their cafeteria, or walk around outside of their cells. Lockdowns could last for a day, a week, or longer.

During lockdown, the inmates at the camp food service would have to make sack lunches and serve those inmates food. I luckily never had to do that because usually the inmates who worked the breakfast and lunch shift would serve them.

Also the COs and admins would get more uptight and strict. There was a riot at the FCI because the inmates were mad about the fact that all camp and FCI inmates had to wear boots from 7 a.m. to 4 p.m. unless they were at rec or coming home from work. FCI inmates got pissed, and they destroyed the yard and the cafeteria, from what I heard. We had to be in the dorm, not in our squares, but we couldn't go outside until told otherwise. I was still working at the powerhouse, and we got called off early from work because the COs in charge of the powerhouse jobs had to go to the FCI. They counted us camp inmates at 1:00 p.m. and again at 3:30 p.m. with the 4:00 p.m. count afterward. There were three counts in three hours. At the 4:30 p.m. dinner, we were freed to have dinner and go back to regular activities.

The lockdown luckily didn't affect my work ethic or my job status. Other camp inmates made lunches for the FCI. The library and other rooms were still open as scheduled. It did, however, affect the institutional movies. For the whole three weeks of lockdown, there were no weekend movies.

Another time, the FCI was on lockdown because of a fight at the yard. Three helicopters dropped down at the FCI, which meant that someone was very seriously hurt. So we were on lockdown until further notice.

Everyone seemed to be sold on that $100 per month working at the FCI. But I remember people getting $3 to $4 for that whole month and having had to fight to get it. Some campers did make $100 per month during lockdown. Plus I heard everyone ate very well because they made homemade quesadillas and whatever they wanted. Unfortunately, camp inmates would be strip-searched before coming back to the dorms.

I found out from the prison nurse who came every day to dispense pills that the lockdown was because thirty southsiders stomped on two of their own. He didn't go into details, but he mentioned that there were boot prints on the victims' foreheads. He claimed it was the worst he'd seen since someone got stabbed twelve times at the same FCI several years ago.

I think that while I was there, the longest a lockdown lasted was two months.

Job Fair at Camp

There was a voluntary job fair which, it turned out, all camp inmates had to attend. It was held it in the visitors' room.

The purpose of the job fair was to teach the inmates how to conduct themselves at a job fair and how to get the most out of a job fair. Normally people would have been taught interview skills such as what to wear, what questions to ask employers, how to ask those questions, and what to bring.

At the job fair that we had, people walked around and talked. There was no job preparation, no interview techniques, no thirty-second interview, no proper dress instruction, or anything. We just walked around chatting with a few people who were at booths, who gave us inaccurate information and false hopes.

There were fifteen representatives there, mostly from government agencies and halfway houses. Lassen College, the junior college in the area, sent a representative. There were also a few people who gave pamphlets on how to come to job fairs. I thought the whole thing was garbage. I got two nice folders. I also got some information about how we could leave the halfway house earlier. Maybe there was something about the going to the fair that was worth it.

The job fair was useless to me because it was only advertising halfway houses, schools, and job placement services. The job placement services were in Nevada. The halfway houses were in Southern California. The schools were anywhere from Southern California to Northern Nevada. There was a probation officer from Sacramento, but I didn't get to meet him.

All we did was walk around and talk to people who were advertising their halfway houses or their schools.

I spent twenty minutes in that place before I was allowed to leave. I voiced my opinion on the survey sheet.

Prison Camp Education

Education didn't seem too serious to inmates when I was there. I saw a few people struggle to understand the GED book. Other inmates told me that there were inmates who just didn't care to get their GED. If an inmate received his GED in camp, he would be eligible for a grade three pay scale and $20 on his books.

The books that the inmates used for GED class were from the Steck-Vaughn series of GED courses. There was a student version and a teacher's version with the answers. Inmates from the GED class told me that the teacher would hold the class and give a short lesson. Then if the inmate needed help, the teacher or his assistant would help the inmate as much as possible. However, most of hour was just time for the inmates to study and to ask questions.

The inmates who were students there complained that the teachers didn't want to teach. They claimed the teacher was uninterested in teaching the class. Both GED assistants I talked to claimed the teachers didn't care and the students did try. Inmates told me that no inmate had successfully received his GED.

The teachers complained the students didn't want to learn or to work hard to learn. The teacher told me that no student cared about their grades. They just took the class to get out of work and to show proof with the lesson plans or exercises.

I think there was truth on both sides. I heard students and teachers say that they didn't even care about the others. The GED teacher was working on changes to the education system at the camp. He was stressing out every time I saw him. He wanted better books for the inmates and better supplies. Then one day around Christmas, he stopped coming to work. When I left in May 2012, there still wasn't a GED teacher.

The camp received government funding based on the GED students taking the class. I'm not sure how much funding the camp received.

Inmates could get higher education while at Herlong. However, I chose not to attend any college classes. While I had thought I could go to prison camp and get a master's in either marketing or creative writing, after I arrived there was no information readily available about how to get this master's degree. The GED teacher told me that I or my family would have to search for the information on our own time. My mom and I didn't even knew where to begin. The GED teacher wouldn't give me any further advice or direction on the matter. I decided to focus on my novel and books and HVAC. I would have to pay for the classes anyway, according to the teacher, because for some reason the prison or government wouldn't pay for it. The only way I could pay would be if my family put money on my books.

There was a junior college called Lassen College in Susanville, California. They had a deal with Herlong Prison to help inmates get associate degrees. Due to budget cuts, the school didn't accept any new students from the camp for the fall semester, which was when I arrived. I would have had to wait until the spring but my sentence was ending in May. In addition, they only offered AA classes, and I already had a BA in English.

In the end, working on this book and my novel made up for not being able to study for a master's.

I also turned down the opportunities to work on other people's homework. I could have gotten plenty of money to do papers for inmates trying to get their degrees. I figured it was not a good use of my time.

In the Library

Time flew by in the library. Eight hours were like four hours, and that was with keeping track of my time because we couldn't miss count or lunches. The library was like another movie room with five DVD/TV combos and a few bookshelves. There was no cable TV in this room, for which I was thankful!

The characters in the library were sometimes cool. Other times, it could be a nut house. Several inmates didn't like to quietly read and write.

The first month I was at camp, there was one regular person in the library, who I'll call Glasses. In an eight-hour period, we might talk about thirty minutes. He was studying his Bible and making business plans for when he got home five years later. That was perfect for when I wanted to put my headphones on and get my work done. At times another writer would come in for an hour at a time, or one of the pastors would come and do some work. It wasn't a nut house until after inmates came back from work. At about two-thirty, the room would fill and people would talk while watching the movies.

However, once I quit the powerhouse, I noticed the place would get annoying after 10:30 a.m. That was the time when most of the inmates were awaking or finished with their morning workout. They had nothing else to do and would get bored. They wanted to watch television and probably didn't have control of the television. So they would come into the library to watch a movie.

I discovered some inmates couldn't handle it when the library was quiet. They would talk or make funny little noises. To stay focused I would put on my headphones and listen to the witchcraft meditation CD or any other type of meditation music. It helped drown out the noises and make me appear unavailable to inmates.

When I didn't put the headphones on, I heard the inmates' nervous habits and loud talking. For example, Blue was a cool dude, but he made loud humming and sucking noises when he really got into his Bible studies, making it difficult for me to concentrate. Another inmate would come in sucking on a lollipop, which sounded like cows grazing. An elderly inmate named Sock would yell "Wow" every time he saw something amazing in a movie. To me, it was like every five minutes. Other inmates would get vocal about the fact there were hardly any new movies in the library, comparing it to their previous institutions where the libraries were updated regularly. As a result, many inmates avoided the library because it was boring to them. They didn't want to just read and write. They wanted to make it a movie room.

A Black Jewish inmate named Cary would come into the library, and he drove everyone crazy. Every time he watched a funny movie, he would burst out laughing. He'd apologize every time he did it, but it came to the point he avoided coming to the library because he was embarrassed about annoying us.

When I didn't wear my headphones, I could hear inmates blast their headphones while eating. Not only did I hear their music or movie clearly through their headphones, but they would eat and talk louder. I made sure that I was there as early as possible to get the best-working DVD player to drown out the sound in the library.

Even when I wore my headphones, I heard most of the noise. However, without my headphones, the inmates assumed that I was available to talk. Without the headphones some inmates didn't understand that I was writing and in a zone. By having the headphones on and the DVD playing, it looked like I was busy. I never understood that.

There were also times when inmates would have passionate debates about politics, policies, and religion. Testimony and Brown would have the most passionate debates. A dude we called Pockets would also get into them. I tried to avoid them whenever possible. Those inmates didn't know what to think of me because of the witchcraft CDs I was listening to. I didn't care because it was the best way to drown everyone out.

Then there was the library orderly, Kells. He thought because he was an orderly, he was like the ruler of the library. Kells was once a driver. He claimed he quit because he was tired of being strip-searched. However, rumor has it that he was less than a year from being released and that the policy was that drivers couldn't be that close to release. He took over the orderly position once I left the powerhouse. He was hardly in the library before he got the job as the library cleaner. At first, he tried to boss everyone around and "make the library better for everyone," as he said. No one listened to him, and they did want they wanted. What was annoying was he would come in and set his stuff in the best seat possible. He would then clean and not return to the library for several hours. When he returned, he packed his stuff and left without ever using the desk.

Kells, like some of the inmates mentioned above, kept talking and rambling about religion and philosophy, even if I asked him not to or I wasn't paying attention to him.

Maybe that was a way to stop me from getting the best seat in the house. We battled for it, and he started staying in the library after cleaning to watch his movies—only to fall asleep minutes into the movie. I soon gave up the thought, it wasn't worth my time. I just wanted a DVD player that worked. Before I left, the room was down to three DVD players that didn't always work. It was funny trying to tell inmates that a DVD player didn't work and watch them try to fix it by hitting the same button. They used the same cleaning disc I used. They would give me a dirty look before walking out. I would find out that inmates blamed me for the DVD players being broken. They believed that my witchcraft CD damaged it. It also could have been because I played the DVD for over eight hours a day with no break. What really happened was that the COs loaned out the DVD players so that people could watch them in the barber shop, or in the rec room's storage area.

The leisure library had five desks but only three work-ing DVD players. If someone was already using the DVD player, other inmates couldn't use it until the first inmate was done. People like me sat at the desk watching the DVD players and writing at the same time.

Inmates wanted to limit the amount of time that a single person could use a DVD player. I used the DVD player as a CD player to listen to music as I wrote. Now that they were down to three DVD players, they wanted me to free up the DVD player to allow others to watch. I did what I could to make myself comfortable and fruitful.

The library was a good place to watch inmates from afar through the big windows. I could see the front of the barracks from any point in the library. I couldn't hear the conversations at the barracks, but I could watch the inmates pick on each other or just sit on the bench while staring into space. I watched the new white-collar inmates make friends with COs. I watched when there was so much sand that the windows turned brown. I watched the campers stare down attractive female admins and COs. They would make gestures when the COs were out of sight or the childish COs were driving their Gators, the battery-powered golf carts used to get around the facility.

I really liked watching the birds. The sea gulls flew straight if there was no wind. In strong wind, however, they flew backward.

Without Kells there, the library was quiet. YT was there but it felt like he was invisible. I was into my writing, and he was into his thing. I didn't really realize that he was there. When Fake Pastor sat in the library, he would tap his finger so loud that it felt like knocking, and he blasted his headphones to the point where I could clearly hear his music. Other people came in who were uncomfortable with the chairs and seating so they moved the furniture around, bumping, kicking, and making loud noises.

Yawn Man sat in the library crocheting. I talked to him sparingly in the library. He was always good for a conversation, and I talked to him daily.

The dude who took the cake was Psycho T. He was a bitter dude. He complained and mumbled to himself then randomly burst out laughing like he was watching a comedy show for the first time. He made dumb jokes about my broken headphones. He sucked his teeth because he claimed there was something wrong with his wisdom tooth. As he drummed his hands or tapped his feet annoyingly, he burst into laughter again. Every time, he would apologize.

One day, an old man came into the library and got mad at me for popping my knuckles loudly. The funny thing was, he was tapping and making loud shifting noises in his chair. Then he got upset because the people in the library were talking loudly, and he called people dumb for not understanding his point. I just decided to go check my laundry. When I came back, the old man was gone. Yawn Man told me that the old man was talking behind my back.

I just said, "Dude has a long way to go. Hope he has a short sentence."

Then there was Testimony.

He got pissed off at me in the library because I moved his book and writing supplies away from a desk. The rule in the library was that if an inmate was gone for an extended period of time, the next person coming in had the right to move their stuff neatly out of the way and use the desk. We had a problem with inmates setting up their stuff and leaving for hours at a time. I guess somehow when I moved Testimony's stuff, his pen dropped on the floor. To this day, I'm still not sure what happened.

The next thing I knew, he came up to me in the lunch line. He accused me of stealing his pen even though I explained to him what happened. He finished his rant, saying, "For future reference, don't touch my stuff again."

That moment further proved a theory I had about Testimony and other inmates. He was a person who was begging for respect but couldn't get it from the brothers due to his childish ways.

I explained to him that if I was in that same situation again, I would do the same thing.

He then pointed at me, saying, "If you touch my stuff again, I don't care how it's on the desk, we're going to have a problem."

I translated that as he wanted to fight right there. I had to remind myself that my time was too short to deal with him, especially in that manner. I was also thrown off because I had always respected the man, and we were going to fall out over one half of a $2 pack of pens? I lost respect for the man at that point.

From that point forward, he never respected me. He gave me little problems on the dinner line when he came through. He would try to talk down to me, and he made jokes that backfired on him. A few of the brothers told

Testimony to stop picking on me, but he didn't listen. They said that if he had got mad at me like that in a low-security institution, inmates would have beaten him up because it was so stupid.

After about a week or so of that, I walked up to him and said, "Look man, you wanna hate me, that fine. But this childish talking shit is going to stop. Now we can go somewhere and handle it like men, or you can stay on your side and I'll stay on mine." He never responded, but he stopped the childish talking.

Weeks later, Testimony gave me a shitty attitude when I wanted to share the only dictionary in the library. "You know I'm going to be going back and forth using it. So I might just take it," he said.

My response to him was, "Cool."

He never took the dictionary. In fact, he left the library after about fifteen minutes and didn't return.

Regardless of the drama in the library, I had some good times. I had great conversations about religious beliefs, investing, doing business in Africa, or post-camp dreams. If the drama in the library was too much for me, I'd go into the classroom or the food service area.

Writing in the Food Service Area

The food service area was usually silent after five o'clock. Normally it was the best place to avoid all the long conversations and drama. However, I didn't like to be in there too often because that was one of the places where inmates hid contraband. I'd be blamed for anything the COs found unless I gave up an inmate, but I honestly wouldn't know who the contraband belonged to. The other major issue was that because the food service area was considered out of bounds the COs could have given me a shot for being in there. Some inmates used the food service area as a band and music room because of some drama in the arts and crafts room, but that was a minor problem.

Once while I was in there, the CO asked me if I was allowed to be in there. I said, "It depends on the CO. But I can leave. No problem." I started packing my stuff.

The CO said, "Naw, you're not doing anything. Don't get into anything and you're fine."

I held up a draft of my novel. "This is the only thing I'm doing."

He looked at his watch and said, "You got 45 minutes." It was 7:45 p.m. and yard recall was 8:30 that day. I thanked him because, to be honest, I could have gotten a 300-series shot for being out of bounds.

Ultimately, I stayed in the library for my last few months there. Mainly because of the possible problems that could have happened to me. Regardless of the problems the library had, I had a good seat always and people started giving me the space I needed for writing, although it was limited. I still got some good work done.

Writing in Classroom 2

I tried to study in classroom 2. However, that room was reserved for religious studies, inmate-run classes, or GED. So my time in that room was limited.

The first classroom had a bunch of computers, like a computer lab. Anyone caught there would get an out-of-bounds shot. I understood that the computers were broken. However, I did see a class in there one day for teaching computer skills. But it was during work hours and there was little to no participation.

However, classroom 2 was always closed off when not in use because the GED tutor, who was also a inmate, didn't let people in the room. Everyone was a little scared of him.

Out of the blue, he got sent to the hole. He was only thirteen months from finishing a twenty-five-year sentence for first-time drug charges. Supposedly they shipped him out because he had eleven points before he got in trouble for having too many magazines in his locker. That one shot raised his total to twelve points, making him ineligible for camp. As far as I know, he went to another prison. Another rumor claimed he cussed a few administrators and others claimed that it was a routine witch hunt. It was his departure that freed up classroom 2.

After no one had been in that classroom for three days, I figured out that the room was perfect for me from 8 a.m. to 10:30 a.m., after which time I would go to the library. If that didn't work, I would go to the food service area.

No one came into classroom 2 because the television cord for cable reception was missing. The only people who used the room were studying or doing religious rituals. And it helped to put on the witchcraft CD. The few people who heard me listen to it while writing thought I was strange, which is usually funny to me because all it did was relax my mind as I wrote. It helped me focus on one thing instead of several things.

The bad thing about being in the classroom 2 was that there was no natural light and there was no way to get a nice breeze. That was the reason people in the library didn't want to study in the classroom 2. All I saw were the white brick walls and the window showing inmates and admins walking past and watching me write. Though there was a clock right above me, if someone wasn't around to remind me of count time, I lost track of time writing. It was quieter for the most part because the library crew didn't want to be in that room.

Regardless of the problems I had in the library, I did find myself more productive in there during the times inmates didn't talk loud. I did miss the big window and the sunlight.

While working in the classroom, I took breaks to do laundry, or I took a walk. I also had to yield the room to other inmates during their religious studies, educational studies, or worship because the room was designated for those purposes, although I would prefer to stay in one spot and get as much done as possible when I started writing. At times, I'd find myself writing and reading in the barracks, which was the one place I tried to avoid because I slept there and I didn't want dumb conversations.

Another problem with classroom 2 was the television use. After I'd been writing for some time in classroom 2, an inmate found the missing cable cord for the television. Suddenly, some inmates got upset because they believed I was stopping them from watching the television. Usually these would be the inmates who didn't have a full-time job and couldn't find anything to do but watch television. There were four televisions in the barracks plus three television rooms, a television in the rec room, and another in the utility room. Inmates didn't care about the room's assigned uses. They yielded to religious and inmate-run classes but made a huge uproar when people wanted to study.

What started the issue and got me involved was the fact that the cable cord was missing. Long before I started writing in the room, someone kept hiding the cord because the GED teacher and his assistant didn't want inmates to watch television in that room. They only wanted inmates there who were studying. However, inmates always hid things in the same places, so other inmates would find the cord and hook up the television. That situation carried on for years.

Inmates who found themselves bored didn't cared that I was studying or writing. They didn't want me hogging up, as they referred to it, the television from

6:30 a.m. to 8:30 p.m. and only getting up for a one-hour lunch break, dinner break, and count. All they wanted was their television.

One inmate, whom I'll call Pulitzer, blamed me for stealing and hiding the cord. It was almost time for *60 Minutes,* a program that Pulitzer claimed to have watched every week since he had been in camp. He even mentioned that one of the Blacks came and enjoyed the program with him. But I put the room back the way I found it. I had nothing to do with the cord. He blamed me because I was always in there.

After some friendly small talk, he snapped, "Why did you steal the cord?"

I said, "Um, the cord is there in the television and it's been there as long as I can remember."

"Well, it came up missing."

"Well, the cord is there and it's been there. Go ahead and watch your program."

Pulitzer said, "Okay, cool." When I told him I was staying to study, he said, "That's not a problem. My problem is you hid the cord and didn't tell me." He continued to ramble, most of which I tuned out.

Pulitzer was a White dude who'd been down most of his life. At the time, he was halfway through his ten-year bid. He also mentioned during that conversation that he was trying to help the Asians to have a television because the Whites had one television to themselves and they shared another television with the Asians. Also the Asians had their own television as well to themselves. The Mexicans had two televisions and the Blacks had two televisions. He was trying to give the Asians another television so that every race has two televisions. It seemed as if he wanted me to get out of the room so the Asians could have their own television, which would give the Whites two of their own televisions. I was too short to worry about these problems

Televisions were very important to inmates when I was there. I think it was because it was their way of keeping up with the outside world. Maybe it was because it was the perfect escapism.

He also did the same line of questioning with two other Blacks, both of whom almost erupted into a shouting match. My friend wanted to clock him. Of course, he didn't, but it was still annoying. Pulitzer blamed YT for taking the cord. He also said that I was different ever since I started hanging out with YT. I used to be a good person but now I did whatever YT said.

Because of all that drama, I decided to stop going into classroom 2. It wasn't worth me continuously fighting for a place to write when I had other options. Also I started working out with YT in the morning. Because of the length of the morning workout, I wouldn't be the first one in classroom 2, so I couldn't get the room to myself. After the workout, I worked in the library.

The Sports Television Room

The sport television room was where the sports games were on most of the time. If there were no sports, we would watch ESPN or whatever television programs the inmates wanted to watch. Most of the inmates in that room were the Blacks, and a few other races came into the room from time to time. We got to see all of the Raider games because we were just outside of the blackout zone. I thought that was a nice perk because I'm a Raiders fan. Other shows we would watch would be *Desperate Housewives, The Good Wife,* and *The Young and the Restless.* Also, depending on who would be in the room, some Blacks would watch BET or daytime court programs. Other nationalities would watch similar shows. However, the Blacks would keep it on the channels we enjoyed watching. It wasn't a "Black" television room, but most non-Blacks didn't ask to change the channel in that room.

During Raider games I would make small bets. I minimized my bets as much as possible. I didn't want to be in a position where I owed more than I could afford. I usually bet on my Raiders or the Kings, if they were on TV. I will say that Tim Tebow when he played for the Broncos cost me about five ice creams, hundreds of push-ups, a hundred and fifty sit-ups, and a hundred jumping jacks.

I would make bets with something I had already, like ramen noodles or push-ups or sit-ups. NB, who was from Boston, was a Patriots fan. I have to admit it was nice having that win. When Tebow was on the Broncos, I lost five bets to Frank and NB since they knew that the Raiders would lose and I didn't like Tebow. Every time Tebow would win a game Frank would scream "Tebow, Tebow!" then he'd Tebow me, by mimicking Tebow's touchdown prayer by getting on one knee and lowering his head onto his biceps.

On Fridays, Saturdays, and Sundays there would be an institution movie for the camp and the FCI. We would watch movies that were newly released to video such as the *Tron: Legacy*, *Captain America*, and *Thor*. There was usually one Black film and a Spanish film, or a Spanish-dubbed film. These films would not be available during lockdowns. Unless there was a meaningful play-off game, the camp inmates in charge of the television remote control in the sports television room would play the institution movie instead of the sporting event.

The Blacks at Herlong Camp

About half of the Blacks at the camp were there for drug-related crimes, and the other half were there for white-collar crimes.

At first, I thought that all the Blacks there were tight because I saw us watching television, playing cards, and having a good time together. I would find out differently when I was getting my haircut and chatting with two of the brothers who were in the shop. It turned out that the Blacks weren't as tight as I thought.

Some Blacks were selling out just to be tokens to White folks. They believed Whites, especially the white-collar criminals, gave advice and kickbacks that other Blacks didn't. However, those sellout Blacks got little respect from their people and even less respect from the Whites. Black inmates told me that those token Blacks would only hang with other Blacks to get protection from other races and to get television use, equipment use, or some other prison perk.

One brother named RT ran with the Blacks when he was in the low-security prison. However, when he came to the camp, he didn't want to be around Blacks because they were too ghetto and lived in the past. He wanted to move forward in his life and find a quick way to get ahead. He decided to associate with some of the white-collar White inmates. In exchange for handouts and random hookups, RT got stock advice and information about investing and business. The funny thing was when RT told me about the advice he got, it didn't make sense to me. I think it was because he didn't totally understand the information or he explained it wrong. I would question to myself whether he was really smart enough to understand the information or whether the Whites didn't give him good advice.

I also felt that other Black Christian inmates tolerated non-Christians because they chose not to correct or repent for their so-called sinful ways. At Herlong Camp, there were between twelve and twenty Blacks at any given time, out of an overall population of 100–141 campers. We didn't have enough Blacks for division among ourselves.

Yet, there were some Black Christian inmates, like Testimony, who would all but abandon his brothers in favor of White inmates because they were more godly. In turn, these same Christians complained that more Blacks weren't in the inmate-led churches and services. Testimony was also on that list because he only talked to some Blacks. I think it was because a lot of Blacks didn't like his immaturity. However, Testimony had told me he didn't like what he called the ghettoness of the Blacks and that he learned more from Whites than Blacks. When I asked him to give me specifics, he couldn't tell me any at all. Many of the Blacks made fun of Testimony because they thought he was hen-pecked and did whatever his wife told him. Because he didn't like getting picked on, Testimony hung out with Mexicans and Whites more than with the Blacks.

Then there was Fake Pastor, who hung with the Blacks but talked mess about them and didn't care too much about White people either. He strongly believed that man was not created in the image of God and that he was not trying to be like Jesus. He had an AA degree in theology and was working on trying to get his bachelor's and master's in theology. He was taking a correspondence course that allowed him to get both at the same time, so he said. Once he was picking my brain about how to write. He was pretty happy because he got 150 words down in the year-plus that he had been there. He said it wasn't the best environment for writing. "You agree right, Pyerse?" I just smiled. I would later tell him I wrote 150 words by accident and that I usually did about a thousand a day. He unfortunately felt the need to prove he was just as hard as everyone else. I think he let his displeasure of the camp bring him down.

For the most part, the other Blacks got along with me because I was myself. I always thought about the brothers if I had extras from the kitchen, knew something that would benefit them, and didn't cause any trouble. I never had a problem loaning stuff. I took care of my bunky first, and then I'd look out for the other Blacks. If any remained, I'd hook up some of the other races. However, by that time, they would have their own methods of hooking up.

Also, I wasn't usually whining to other inmates. I did most of my complaining and whining in my journal. I had my moments, but I never got out of hand or drove people crazy. I also never really got along with the other races except for the ones in the library or the ones that were good with the Blacks. It was mainly because those races wanted to focus on being with their race. Some of the other races just wanted to be to themselves for their own reasons.

For the most part, you had two types of Blacks: the ones who studied and worked to make their lives better and the ones who wasted their time in front of BET. The other Blacks that studied or read did so in their bunks or at their jobs when they took breaks.

I also saw about 60 percent of the Blacks really try to work on their post-prison life. These brothers wouldn't watch television all day. They would study for trades or create business plans. They would dive deep into their spirituality and learn about themselves. They would make crafts for their children and learn how to be a better parent. They would focus on working out and eating healthily, whenever possible.

The other types of Blacks at the camp were the ones who wasted themselves in the form of housewife shows, BET, and courtroom shows. These would be the brothers who played cards or dominoes all day and complained about boredom. They were the brothers who worked as little as possible just to avoid work and to get in front of the television.

Most of the brothers from higher institutions would have a hustle. Some brothers would have food from the kitchen and get stamps, while others would make arts and crafts and sell it for tuna or stamps.

Myths About Prison Camp

I understand and respect it when people say that prison camp was easy and not real prison. The longer I stayed there, the more I understood that statement. However, there were things that made it difficult. The false hopes were one of the worst problems.

For instance, there was a piece of paper that claimed that any federal inmate could become federal-bonded felons and/or receive disability or various cash or loans. Sounds amazing right? I was there for about two weeks and suddenly thought that my being in prison was the best thing that ever happened to me.

The paper said that because I was federally incarcerated, I could get up to $300 per month from Supplemental Security Income (SSI). For me, that meant I'd get $5,100 when my seventeen months ended. I could have started a nice business with that money. On top of that, the paper said there was a strong possibility that the Small Business Administration would give federal inmates a loan for up to $50,000, which would be bonded by the federal government.

I honestly tried to take it with a grain of salt, but I couldn't because it sounded like such a good way to get my life back off the ground.

It would turn out that it was a complete lie.

None of the administrators knew of the programs. My family called the 1-800 number, which never worked.

When I got home I found this on the SSI website:

"Social Security and Supplemental Security Income (SSI) payments generally are not payable for months that you are confined to a jail, prison or certain other public institutions for commission of a crime. You are not automatically eligible for Social Security or SSI payments when you are released."

The only way I could get $300 month for being in prison was if I was completely, insanely crazy and my condition was permanent and I couldn't get a regular job or make a living. Only a licensed doctor would be able to prove such a thing. Of course, if I was able to prove all that, I probably would have not written this book or washed dishes.

After I got home, I found no evidence that the Small Business Administration would give inmates any amount of money. I did heard some stories that one person received $300 per month, but it wasn't for every month that he was sentenced to. It was for after he'd been released. Therefore, every month he got $300 for the rest of his life.

Yet some people inside strongly believed these claims and asked questions just like I did. There were even some people who believed that because they'd been down ten years they were going to get an enormous check when they got home.

Early release from prison was the other false hope. Inmates believed that Obama, or whoever was currently in office, would work with Congress to shorten the sentences to free up prison space. Inmates from higher institutions told me they heard that lie since Clinton was in office.

There also was a rumor about reducing the 89 percent mandatory serving time to 50 percent for nonviolent inmates. That also turned out to be false.

The only rumor that turned out to be true was the law reducing the crack sentencing from 100 to 1 to 18 to 1. That law reduced a few inmates' sentences as much as half, or to time served. I saw some inmates who had five more years to go, go home before I did.

Last Days at Herlong

From the last week of April 2012 until my last day at camp on May 7, 2012, I was so distracted with thoughts of how great my life was going to be at the halfway house that I couldn't focus on my writing. For example, I was thinking of the positive aspects that I learned from prison. I dreamed about a special person, my family, my first drink, my first interaction with non-prison people, and my post-prison life.

I remembered talking highly of going to the halfway house and the opportunities that were going to present themselves. I looked over my notebook of post-prison plans and tried to finalize them, as much as possible. It was the point in time when I did the least amount of writing. Some brothers made me some dishes the day before I left.

I joked with NB about leaving my bunk as dirty as possible. I told him I was going to leave dirty under-wear, garbage, and stains in my locker. I even joked about peeing on my bed and leaving it there. He was mad at first because he had a hard time telling whether I was joking. But of course, I cleaned the whole place. I couldn't do that to him.

During that last week, I was approached by so many inmates, especially the ones I didn't talk to the whole time I was there. They would ask me when I was leaving and who was going to get my bunk. At first I would lie and say I was leaving weeks later. Other times I would just ignore them. The closer I got to my release day, the more that inmates would ask me if there was anything of mine they could have. I actually gave most of my stuff away days, even weeks, before I left. I also reduced the number of commissary items I purchased to make sure I didn't have too much stuff on my last day.

I said good-bye to everyone and wished them luck. My last day I spent time with YT, and we laughed at me because I wanted a slice of pizza for my way home. I figured I wouldn't eat for a while so I needed to eat as much as possible while I was there. The camp did give me $20 plus the additional $20 on my books. However, I wasn't sure how much the taxi or other transportation would cost. He still laughed at me because he felt I should had been sick of the prison food.

Also, on my last day, I didn't leave until 11:00 a.m. There was a miscommunication that I was supposed to leave at 9:00 a.m. When I got to Processing and Receiving, the COs were mad because they had to box about forty pounds of my books and clothes. They yelled and complained but I was free. I didn't care, I was leaving.

On my way out, the cashier gave me my money. From there, I got into the van with the town driver, who was a camper, to go to the Reno Greyhound station.

First Day at the Halfway House

On May 7, 2012, I arrived in Oakland at about six o'clock. I tried to get the people at the station to call a taxi for me, but they said a taxi wouldn't come for such a short trip. At the station I fell in a hole that was poorly covered by a cheap piece of wood. I couldn't call anyone because I didn't have any type of phone. I started walking to the halfway house while carrying that box of books and clothes. I hoped that I would figure out the directions as I went along. Then I got lost. I thought the halfway house was facing Lake Merritt. I would later remember it was facing the 580 freeway. The only reason I made it to the halfway house was because a nice Black couple took me there. I tried to give them some money, but they didn't want it.

When I arrived at the halfway house, I was thirty minutes late. I was glad and thankful they didn't bust me and send me back for being so late. The staff member told me to sit at the side and wait for him. It was a long wait, which was fine, because it gave me an opportunity to absorb my surroundings. My first thought was that the halfway house was going to be fun and a great way to get started. My second thought was that every staff there seemed heavily stressed and tense.

I sat in the office while they dealt with other residents.

The staff would slowly process me and then they sent me out of the room to watch the television with the residents. The room was entirely Black men watching the playoff game. There were non-Black residents, but they chose to watch the game in their rooms because the Blacks were too loud for them.

I wasn't really into the game. I wanted to shower and get some writing done, but the staff wouldn't let me until they finished processing me. I remembered getting dead tired because the only thing I had eaten all day was the pizza I had back in Herlong.

Around seven o'clock, two federal parole officers came and had a town hall meeting with the residents. The meeting was about we needed to do more to help our progress and get back into society. It was a reminder that we were still in the custody of the Bureau of Prisons. I think that's part of the reason residents continued to call themselves *inmates*.

The officers then took questions and comments from the inmates. The inmates talked about their displeasure about not getting more time outside of the halfway house with their families and admins not caring or being supportive. The POs said they would do what they could but the admins were acting properly under BOP rules and conduct. Of course, they invited us to call them if we had any questions. The meeting ended in about two hours. During that time, I wasn't allowed to get officially processed or to take a shower. I missed dinner because I was late and because of the meeting. Dinner was served at 6:30 p.m. and 7:30 p.m.

There was no outside food because people hadn't

done their chores on time. The halfway house provided food for all the residents because the residents were still considered property of the United States government. Any food from outside the kitchen was considered a privilege, meaning something that was not really needed to make the residents' lives better. Whenever the staff were upset at us and needed to punish us, they would revoke privileges such as allowing residents to have outside food within the halfway house. We had to eat the food that was there. The food was catered locally. I thought the camp food tasted better, but I ate it to save as much money as possible.

Because the residents didn't complete their chores to the staff's satisfaction, all outside passes, except for volunteering, employment, and requests approved by the head director, were revoked. Normally, we were able to get permission to go to the movies or visit family by way of an outside pass. We would just have to fill out a daily itinerary request (DIR), a written request for time outside the halfway house. In most cases, the resident's case manager would have to approve the request before a resident could leave the house. We were usually allowed up to 12 hours outside the halfway house for work. If a resident wanted to volunteer, they would get just enough time to get to and from the location. A request to attend church or to visit religious organizations would require a DIR and be approved by the resident's case manager. Any other outing, such as going home or watching a movie, had to be approved by the head director.

Even after the officers left, the staff still slacked off

in getting me processed. They did things like making their count and finishing their end of shift duties. Their count was simple; they just walked around the house and rooms and checked names off a list. No standing, no IDs, so lieutenants yelling at us.

It took them until 11:00 p.m. to finish processing me. My bed was assigned to me by the head of security. However, I still wanted to shower so I had to wait until damn near midnight to get a towel and soap from the head of security. He was trying to do his job as well as help me out. When I asked him for some detergent, he said, "I'll see what they can do." I didn't care, honestly; I was dead tired. My body was used to sleeping at 10 p.m.

The first room I was assigned to was a six-man room with three other Black men, a White man, and a Pakistani man. For the most part, they were cool toward me. I was very standoffish that day because I was dead tired. Later, I would be standoffish because I wanted more privacy. There was one closet, three dressers, a television, and a desk, like the ones in high school. My roommates normally didn't sleep until two in the morning. Instead, they played music all night or talked on the phone. My bunky watched television without headphones so he had to play it loud enough to hear over everyone else's music. There was no way I was going to be the new guy who was going to tell them what to do, because that was so annoying and a quick way to lose respect.

In addition, I was supposed to have two small drawers and a larger one in the dresser. My bunky would have the same. He took my two little drawers and claimed it was "policy." Instead of fighting back, I just put my

182

belongings in the one large drawer and left the rest in the box.

As much as I hated camp, at that moment all I wanted to do was go back to it. However, I figured, it would get better.

My First Weeks
at the Halfway House

One of the house rules that bugged me the most was that I was not allowed to leave the house for the first three days. I couldn't even get my one hour of recreation time, or rec time. That was the time residents could do anything they wanted to, as long as they were back in one hour. Most residents used that time to purchase their hygiene or get food, when outside food was allowed. Some residents ran errands close by. Because I couldn't leave to buy my hygiene, I had to borrow some from my roommates.

Four days later, that Friday, I still didn't have my orientation completed and hadn't talked to the job developer. These two meetings were requirements to leave the house, even for an hour. Because of that, I wanted to go back to camp. At least there I could do something. At the halfway house I just sat around listening to other people's problems and the same prison and hood stories I heard at camp. I usually didn't share those types of stories so I found it hard to relate at times.

Of course, I usually took my time opening up to people. It was harder to open up because I wanted more space from everyone and a quiet place to write. The room had one desk, which was fine when I was alone. But my bunky didn't work and he blasted the television when he was there. And my roommates would play music and talk so loud, I couldn't focus on reading or writing.

Luckily, on the following Tuesday I was there, my case manager allowed my parents to come and get my books from the camp and give me the hygiene and clothes I really needed for job interviews. They also gave me an iPhone 3G and took my books from prison back to their house. My iPhone was taken from me because it hadn't been approved by the head director. He would approve of it a few days later. Because my parents didn't come during visiting hours, I was only allowed to see them for a second. It was the first time I saw my stepfather in a year. Although I was glad to see him and my mom, I didn't like the fact I could only shake his hand and talk to him for five minutes.

Before they left they reminded me of how far I had come and that it was only a few more days and then I could go back to Sacramento. They told me I had a place to stay with them, free of charge until I got on my feet. That conversation, as quick as it was, made me feel a lot better. It reminded me that all I had to do was tough it out at the halfway house for a few weeks then I could leave for Sacramento and get on my feet.

During that same week, I had called my PO to ask to go back to camp. He never returned my call. However, a day after I called him, I got my meeting with the job developer. The job developer gave me instructions and permission, as in a daily pass, to get my social security card and license. More importantly, I got permission to have my one-hour rec time and went to the store to get some more hygiene. Suddenly, I started seeing that there were some things I could work out by being here. I called my PO to make sure that there wasn't any confusion or mistakes.

It was also during this week that I talked to my case manager. He was an African named Mr. Jacob. He informed me that I wasn't able to return to Sacramento until I reached level four, which meant basically I had to have a job. However, I would still have to come to the halfway house to attend the mandatory classes and for random drug tests. If they were to call me in for a drug test I would have two hours to get to the halfway house or it resulted in a failed test. Mr. Jacob informed me, like so many staff members had before him, that if I failed one test, I would be shipped back to prison, with no guarantee that I would go back to a camp, with a new charge and possibly additional time on my sentence. Also, I would be forced to pay the halfway house for a bed as if I were still at the house, which was 25 percent of my income. At that time, I still was considering going back to Sacramento because I just wanted to go home and I was emotionally exhausted from the prison culture.

My Opinion of the Staff and Some of the Halfway House Rules

Rumor had it that the reason the halfway house was so strict was because of a death just outside the halfway house a few years before. Because of that death, they had to strengthen the rules and be stricter or risk losing their contract with the federal government. The government gave the halfway house money for every resident plus for every resident who completed classes taught by the halfway house.

Other than that, it was like camp except that I could use my time to work on my novel or type up résumés. I had to do that on my one-hour recreation time at the library.

The television in the living room was only on from 6 to 9 a.m. and from 5 to 10 p.m. There was no television otherwise. The living room was for job research. They had a few job books and the yellow pages down there. We were not allowed to use cell phones in the living room at any point in time. The books in the living room were not allowed to leave the area. Even so, I had one of the EDD books in my room. I was trying to make that process work. If we needed a computer to do job research, we would have to go to the library or get a day pass. However, we needed to do volunteer work or have a job to get a day pass.

All the things in the halfway house seemed to be done to please the government instead of trying to find what kind of help we needed as individuals. We had to get jobs that would please the government, not jobs that would better us as men and women. My case manager made it clear to me that he was only doing enough to get me on my feet by following the GEO Care and government guidelines. He was not concerned with trying to help me use my degree or get established in Sacramento.

The staff's primary task was to keep the contract with the government. If helping the residents would keep the government contract, then that would be the help that we would get. Otherwise, residents would be told that their request would not be handled or approved.

My case managers were horrible. As mentioned earlier, Mr. Jacob was my first case manager. He seemed to want to only do his job and nothing more than that. He was also annoyed at me for asking questions. I wasn't trying to annoy him, honestly. I was just excited and full of optimism. Though I was always somewhat optimistic, it finally seemed like I could get something moving in life.

Yet he was annoyed at me when I asked him to give me daily work passes, which was his job, because the temp agency gave me additional hours. He told me that he would not allow me to accept any job offers unless it came with a 24-hour notice. I don't know his reasons, but he seemed to hate to do anything extra for me. I don't know if it was an attack on me or he was the type of employee who felt he was underpaid so he only did just enough to keep the job. Mr. Jacob told me that the agency was using me and I needed to stop kissing up to them. When I told him I just wanted the money, he said, "Again, you're not getting a pass unless it you give me a 24-hour notice." Luckily, that didn't hurt my job offers from the temp agency.

When he went on vacation during my second month there, my new case manager was a White man who was known to be annoying and to power trip. He was one of those people who seemed to love his power and joked about it all the time. I felt like he was bragging about his riches to poor people. Our personalities just didn't mesh. He tried to have fun and make me smile. I wasn't going to smile, I wanted to go home. Once he realized I wasn't trying to have fun with him, he was just strict and to the point with me. However, I didn't get a lot of favors from him, which was a fair trade-off for his leaving me alone.

The second month I was there, they hired a few new people after a staff worker walked out without notice. Even with additional help, those employees and case managers had to help with the front desk and work overtime because the staff took vacation and called in sick. The new employees were quickly annoyed and overly stressed, which only made it more difficult for residents to get passes or anything that required permission. The other issue was that the entire staff would gossip and complain about their bosses, coworkers, and their pay to the residents and their guests.

One of the new hires was a skinny man named Ty. He walked and worked slow. The residents thought of him as soft and gay. I thought he was just soft and whiny. Ty started power tripping as soon as he was hired and was overly picky with housework. A few residents put him in his place, after which Ty would just keep to himself and stare back at us with evil eyes.

Another staff worker I didn't like was Miss W. She talked mess and called some of the Blacks by the n-word. She was Mexican and acted ghetto. Some brothers liked that controlling and nagging, saying that it reminded them of their women and mothers at home. My mother was never like that so I couldn't relate. Miss W was loud, whiny, and complained about how she hated it there and how she was ready to quit. Yet she showed no signs of quitting as far as I could see. I just minded my own business. She was cool to me and referred to me as "Dandridge."

The gentleman who was head of security didn't give me too many problems because I rarely saw him. He would just say hi and bye to me, and that would be it.

Ms. Salters, another Black lady, was in charge of the community service and volunteer program at the house. I got the impression she never really cared if I did community service or not. I had a community service job where I helped a church with cleaning their gym and parking lot. I got free bus passes from Salters. I found out a week later that I was only allowed two free passes and only one was allowed for the community service. The second weekly pass I got from the job developer, but that was for applying at Acrobat Outsourcing in

San Francisco. Acrobat Outsourcing was a temporary employment agency that specialized in culinary and restaurant staffing. They gave me about twenty to forty hours of work a week. I worked on ships, at baseball games, and at weddings.

The bus pass issue happened during the two weeks that I didn't have income. Salters told me there was no way to get additional passes. The job developer wouldn't allow me to get another pass until I got a job, but I needed to use it for job-related activities. I asked Salters if I could have a community service job that was in walking distance.

"Well, no, because you already have a community service position," she said. When I asked her if I could just change jobs, she said, "No, I don't do that. If I do that for you I'd have to do it for everyone. I just don't do that."

So I only completed two community service jobs, but I didn't need any additional community service to please the halfway house. I just wanted to do as much outside work as possible to stay out of the house.

I think she wasn't tripping about my not doing community service because community service jobs and employment both could be programming.

She did complete my DIR for July 23–27, 2012, and acted as if she did a huge favor for me. Honestly, at first she tried to tell me she didn't do them. After she accused me of not knowing what I was talking about, another case manager told her, "Yes, you are doing the DIRs."

"Oh well, I didn't know," she snapped. "Email me your job order from Acrobat."

It took two days for her to sign the DIRs. That was my last interaction with Ms. Salters.

I decided to stay at the Oakland halfway house instead of going back to Sacramento to look for a job. It was too complicated. After I was down to about seven or eight weeks left, I figured I could handle that much time at the halfway house. Second, if I got a job in Sacramento, I'd have to commute back and forth for a month, five days or even seven days a week, until my home confinement date, which was five weeks later. Even after that home confinement date, I'd still have to return to Oakland for random, mandatory drug tests and the house classes. The classes and drug testing superseded my employment obligations, even if I was out of town. I'd still have to pay the halfway house fee of 25 percent of my gross income. It wasn't worth it. It wouldn't be worth the money for me to commute back and forth.

I had cordial relationships with three employees there. One of them was a Black employee named RL. He was quiet and never bothered me. He just did his job, from what I could tell. He got along with most of the residents and did what he could to help us. He was the one who allowed me to come late my first day at the halfway house. The other two were not really super nice to me, but they didn't bother me. I also had a cordial relationship with the job developer, which I'll talk about later.

The head director of the halfway house had been there for years. He was always concerned about me not being happy or grateful while I was there. I just wanted as much distance from these superiors as possible. I felt like property when I talked to these people. I also saw him as a corporate puppet who had the nerve to be self-righteous. It was annoying that I had to vocalize my frustration or offer suggestions because he wanted me to do what they felt was in my best interest. Looking back, I think it's possible that they could have cared, but not enough to make me change my opinion of them.

Programming and Workshops in the Halfway House

Programming in the halfway house was similar to the camp, which was anything that would help the resident change or aid them in their path to be a productive member of society. Residents could program by going to religious services, gaining and maintaining employment, volunteering in the community, and attending federally mandated workshops and programming classes.

What I didn't like about the classes and workshops was that they were a higher priority than my job or religious practices. Of course, the house got money from the government for every resident that took a class and every resident that passed a class. All residents had to be in that program, regardless of their felony, for all nine weeks, plus other four programming classes. If I had a religious obligation the same day as my mandatory classes, I would not get permission to attend my religious obligation. In Herlong I would have gotten permission to go to the religious meeting as long as there was no security risk.

Every time I went to a class, I felt that the teachers were giving us only enough helpful information to please the government and not go above and beyond that to help the residents. The classes were taught by the staff and assistant director, and always seemed rushed. Personally, I didn't mind because I wanted it over as soon as possible. Most of the time, the students really didn't want to be in the class so they would just talk enough to make it look as if they participated.

In one job development class, the job developer was discussing how a resident should mention their weaknesses during a job interview. She taught us to mention that we have weaknesses and that we have strengths. I had previously been taught never to mention the word *weakness* but instead to say, "These are areas that are challenging to me and things I would like to improve."

After the class, I mentioned this statement to her. She said, "Well, you can't expect those guys to understand that. They just need the basics."

During a mandatory AA meeting, the instructor focused most of his time talking about his troubles with alcohol and his faith in Christ. He talked about how he woke up drinking VO and 7Up. He apologized continuously about his alcoholism and the people he hurt. He then repeatedly told us how much he loved each and every resident. Though I was proud of him for turning his life around, I just wrote some notes down as other residents tossed and turned in their seats. I felt as if he was trying to promote AA services and beat a dead horse.

Then there was the transition skills class. It was a nine-week mandatory class taught by the assistant director and followed the *Transition Skills* workbook developed by The Change Companies.

The whole book, consisting of forty-one pages, was written in typical BOP workbook eighth grade reading language. I was told that it promoted the policies of BOP while looking like they were helping us. It was supposed to help inmates and residents transition to the real world, deal with the challenges that felons are presented with, and be productive in society. The topics the workbook covered included social skills, decision-making skills, employability, money management, transportation, health, family responsibilities, and basic understanding of the law. I think some residents got something out of it. However, it did little for me because I already knew a lot of the material covered.

I completed the book in two days by filling in random answers. The teacher never checked to see if the answers were correct because, as he said, "There are no incorrect answers." If a resident didn't have his section completed, the whole class would have to wait until he finished the section in the workbook before class was dismissed.

I felt the book was more about proving to residents that returning home from prison was going to be hard and to be prepared for the difficulty. I would have much preferred to be given solutions on making the return easier. The book explained that some relationships will be lost because of the time in prison camp, which actually happened to me. My solution to the problem was to find new friends who respected and understood my experience and allowed me to be myself. The book told residents that adjusting would be difficult but didn't give them any optimism on making new relationships.

The other issue I had was that since it was written at an eighth grade level, I felt as if the book and the teacher was talking down to me. However, I had to remember that some residents, even some older than me, didn't have GEDs. However, I couldn't shake the notion that maybe if they talked to the residents like adults who could learn complex ideas if given a chance, they wouldn't think of themselves as dumb.

It wasn't that people were getting the best job training or opportunities to get that job. Residents were allowed to go *only* to the One-Stop Career Center to look for a job, but people in the whole area went there begging for a job. There wasn't enough time to utilize those services in the time allowed.

Advantages of the Halfway House

I have to admit, however, that there were a few advantages to being at the halfway house. It gave me the chance to save money to get my apartment and some extra play money for when I came home. I got a chance to get my driver's license renewed.

The biggest bonus was I got to transfer my job to the Sacramento branch. I think it would have been much easier to do these things in Sacramento because I had the car already and that was where I was going to return.

Working During the Halfway House Stay

Employment for residents was considered to be a privilege, not a right. However, it was hoped and expected that residents got jobs. The jobs were another source of income for the halfway house. They took 25 percent of the resident's gross, or pre-tax, income.

As soon as I got my job, I was at a level four. Although to be honest, I'm still not sure how I advanced through the levels. I don't know if I ever was on level two. I don't know if I skipped a level. My case manager didn't keep me updated with my progress during our meetings.

Before I could accept an assignment from Acrobat, I would have to fill out a DIR. I had to give my DIRs to my case manager, or whoever was approving DIRs, twenty-four hours prior to the event requested. If these DIRs were work-related, they were usually approved. The approved DIR would tell me what time I was allowed to leave the house and the time that I had to return. Usually, I would get approved for the number of hours I was scheduled to work plus an hour or so for travel. It was very important that I returned within the time periods allowed by the halfway house. Otherwise, I would lose work privileges. Yes, work at that halfway house was considered a privilege, even though the house needed the resident income to operate.

My main transportation was BART and the bus. At first, I was confused by BART stations and stops and when to get off that train, so I was late to my first two assignments and getting back to the house. The staff wrote me up and passed it on to the assistant director for further disciplinary action. However, because he took longer than three days to discuss the write-up with me, halfway house policy didn't allow him to give me any disciplinary action.

At first I was trying to get two jobs and work eighty hours. I figured I had more freedom working than being in the halfway house. The only sure way out of the halfway house was to work. However, I was too tired after most of my shifts. Plus, I was only allowed to be out of the house for a maximum of twelve hours. It didn't matter if the client wanted me to work sixteen hours overtime, I better be back in the house within twelve hours or within the time I was allowed to be out.

Working gave me the opportunity to upgrade my quarters. Besides getting into the two-man room, the other major advantage was that I got out of household chores. I used to clean the bathrooms downstairs or whatever restroom the staff needed cleaning. The cleaning responsibilities went to the residents who didn't pay rent. Also, if I needed to get a day pass, if I was working my request was more than likely to get accepted.

The major advantage of working for the Acrobat agency was the free food. The majority of the assignment I ate whatever the guests ate. I ate everything from seafood and steaks to ball game sausages. When I was able to bring food back from my job assignment, I gave it to the residents that I got along with. Normally I didn't have anything to bring back. Plus, I got an additional meal at the halfway house if I was still hungry. The kitchen would be closed for residents who'd already eaten. However, it was open for residents who worked late.

The New Room, Roommates, and Other Housemates

Around my second month at the halfway house, I got the opportunity to move into a two-man room for no additional charge because I was working over thirty-five hours a week. I'm not sure if working thirty-five hours or more was the actual reason, but it was what the head of security, who assigned the rooms to residents, told me. It was one of the perks of working while in the halfway house. There were only about eight of these rooms, mostly on the third floor, but three rooms were on the second floor. They had a single bunk bed, television, desk, closet, and dresser. The biggest problem I had was the window in the room. I loved the view overlooking the Bay Bridge. However, directly below residents smoked once an hour, and the smoke blew up to my window. The combination of two to fifteen residents smoking made it seem like they were smoking in my room.

Because my room was on the third floor, I didn't have to deal with all the drama downstairs. All the residents that were loud were outside my door. Though it was very hot upstairs, I stayed at work as much as possible, so the heat didn't bother me. Just outside my door were three bunks where six residents slept. They slept in a open loft area with no doors. There was one restroom on this floor. At times the restroom would be used by residents taking a shower, using the restroom, talking on his cell phone, or smoking after the patio closed at 9:30 p.m. Residents who smoked would blow the cigarette smoke into the vent to "prevent the smoke from stinking up the restroom." Sometimes they would sit on their beds and smoke out the window if the bathroom was unavailable.

My first bunky was creepy, needy, and talkative. He was at least twenty years my senior and felt he had to take care of me because I was young, at least compared to prison years. He spent fifteen years in prison for drug possession and selling. Because his experience in prison was longer than mine, he felt entitled to be respected. I gave it to him, but it was mainly to eliminate an unnecessary alpha dog grudge match. Plus, he was getting released in a few weeks, so there was no need to cause unnecessary tension.

However, he felt the need to remind me of what he felt I needed to do. He would make sure that I put in applications for a job. He would make sure that I laid my clothes out for the next day and got my dinner on time. The most annoying thing he would do was talk to me about his personal problems with his last bunky and his family. I tried to humor him and politely get him to stop. I even tried to bury my face in Facebook on my phone. However, it was less annoying to just let him keep talking until he was done as I nodded a few times.

I also found it difficult to do any writing while he was in the room because he stared at me and interrupted.

"Young Dandridge," he'd say, sounding so creepy.

"Yes?"

"You okay, young Dandridge? You're kind of quiet."

"I'm fine."

This exchange would happen several times a week.

My second bunky was quieter. He and I talked, but I was usually at work when he worked. When I was in the room, he stayed to himself and watched old television shows, which was ideal for me.

I helped a few residents with their résumés, but nothing long and extensive. Once in a while I would pitch in for food, but I tried to avoid that because I wanted to save my money for my release.

Last Day of the Halfway House

Leading up to my last day, I worked like crazy, slept as long as possible, and jumped on Facebook to escape the madness of the house. I would keep trying to write, but it wasn't the right atmosphere and I needed to do things to get home. Four weeks before I left, my case manager ordered me to pay the house about $250 in rent. Paying that would allow me to no longer pay weekly to the house. I did so reluctantly because at the time I thought it was too much. It turned out that I might have saved a few dollars because I got more hours during my last few weeks than the previous weeks. I spent a lot of time trying to get job interviews in Sacramento, but that didn't work because I wasn't able to meet them in a short amount of time.

My last day at the halfway house started out uneventfully. Before my bunky left for work, I shook his hand and we wished each other good luck. Afterward, I packed everything in my single suitcase and walked down to the living room. The house was watching the news so I waited until eight in the morning. At that time, I walked to the counter, signed some paperwork, and walked out the door for the last time. I didn't ask for a last meal. I didn't even say bye to anyone else. I just left.

Most residents would wait for a ride to come get

them. I just wanted to get the hell out of there as fast as possible. I walked to the bus stop and waited for my nine-thirty bus. As I waited, I chatted on Facebook and called a few people.

A few hours later, I saw the signs for Sacramento. I have to admit, seeing my home town for the first time in fifteen months seemed surreal and pleasant at the same time. I was moved when I was able to see downtown Sacramento from a few miles away because even though I wasn't home yet, it felt like I was home.

At about noon, my stepfather picked me up at the Greyhound station. We caught up during the drive home and then I went and started taking care of my own personal errands. When my mom came home, I took care of some business with my car. I think I went out drinking with friends and family.

I have to admit that once I got past all the hellos and seeing everyone for the first time, it started to feel as if I had never gone to prison camp or the halfway house.

Supervised Release

As soon as I was released from the halfway house I was placed on supervised release, which I also call probation (though technically there's no such thing as federal probation). I had three days to report to my federal probation officer. I was trying to reach her on the first day out of the halfway house, but she told me to enjoy the weekend and talk to her on Monday. Meanwhile, I moved back into my parents' home and secured my job with Acrobat in Sacramento.

After a weekend full of celebrating and catching up with friends and family, I met my first probation officer. She immediately had me take a drug test, which I passed with flying colors. She then asked me several questions to make sure that I wasn't talking to other felons or in a place with weapons.

When she asked me about my plans, I told her that I wanted to start a Black news website called MyBlack-News.net and make revenue from ads and affiliate marketing. She was okay with the idea, but she wanted me to have a more concrete job. She gave me plenty of time to find a real job and had no problem with me continuing to work for Acrobat.

I did inform her that I was looking for an apartment because my parents were moving to my grandmother's home to save up for a home purchase. My grandmother watched children and it would compromise her business if a felon lived with her.

Because I was moving out of her area, the probation officer decided not to have me pay restitution until she transferred me to another PO. In the meanwhile, I would have to report any travel plans I had outside of my district and any involvement with law enforcement.

My district was the eastern district of California, which was everything east of Solano County, south of the Oregon border, west of the Nevada border, and north of Fresno. If I was to take a quick daylong trip to the Bay Area or outside my district, I would be required to call her to leave a message before I was free to go. If I had plans that were longer than a day, she would have to talk to the federal probation officer in that city, examine the hotel or home I was staying in, and then approve my plans. It could also require the telephone number of the individuals who would be accompanying me. Because I didn't want the government to have my friends' numbers in their files, I avoided long trips.

The next week I moved into my apartment. The PO came in took a quick look at my small studio, examined my car, and went away. She mentioned that she would need a key for the gate and one for my apartment, but she'd let the new PO handle that responsibility.

In October 2012, I got my second and last PO. I talked to him briefly over the phone and he instructed me to turn in my monthly report by mail or in person. I mailed the first one to him. For the second, I wanted to turn in the report personally. When I talked to the clerk at the parole office, he asked if I wanted to see my PO. I said yes and the clerk walked back to give my report to my PO. Minutes later, I was casually talking to my PO about my job situation. At that time, I was still working for Acrobat, but I was getting ready to be hired on by Bon Appétit to wash dishes at William Jessup University in Rocklin. He was pleased with that news and allowed me to check in electronically. He also required that I pay $25 a month until my restitution was fully paid. My restitution was $72,000.

Afterward, I would hardly see my PO. He came to the studio I was renting, then he visited my parents' home when I moved back home. I didn't take a drug test until July 2014, and that was just before I was released from supervised release.

He did require me to report any travel plans with him. I wasn't allowed to leave the district unless he gave me verbal permission. One day I asked if I could go to Oakland to support my friend's spoken word event. He allowed me to go, but he started to ask a few questions about who my friend was and how often I attended the events. Because of that questioning, I chose to avoid going outside of my district. I just didn't want to take the chance of him asking for a friend of mine's number. My main concern was having the government in my friends' business. It would have felt like my dirty laundry was on them.

Other than that, the PO didn't bother me at all. He seemed like he really didn't need to talk to me. That's what I wanted. I was told by inmates that if a PO was on a felon's back a lot, then he was looking for a reason to send that felon back to prison or the halfway house. My PO knew I was trying to stay productive, and I kept paying on my restitution. I wasn't his biggest concern.

Readjustment

I would say that the biggest problem after leaving the halfway house was not dealing with the discrimination or social backlash, it was that I didn't advance as far as I would have liked as fast as I would have liked.

My plan was to get the first job I could, no matter whether it was fast food or a state job, and live as cheaply as possible until I was able to start my own business.

I was thinking that once I got home, my news site would be highly successful. Although I got tons of traffic, the problem I had was I couldn't generate what I thought was favorable income. I would later find out that my method of acquiring news articles and segments violated several copyright laws and I was basically stealing. In a panic, I quickly shut the site down.

I then started blogging about my prison experience and finishing one of the novels I started in camp called *Crime and Punishment*. For whatever reason, I found it difficult to write after getting off work. That book was still in the editing process at the time this book is being written. I thought I had a finished project until I would look at it again and find typos and other major grammatical mistakes.

At the advice of a friend and marketer, I started this book. This book took me about eight months to complete. I thought it would take about three months to convert my journal notes into a publishable book. I think impatience got the best of me because I got upset at myself for not getting this book done in two to three months. I felt like I was slacking.

That feeling of slacking or being lazy would be a continuous problem during my two years on supervised release. I didn't want to wash dishes any longer. I was blessed to have a job. However, I wanted to be a writer or at least use my skills in web development and writing to make a living. I was tired of dealing with bosses. I remembered feeling like a failure when a plan of mine didn't work the way I planned.

It was also depressing that I couldn't find a quality job. I tried applying for the state, county, and federal jobs. My efforts would result in rejection letters or no responses at all. I was also frustrated that I couldn't get more hours with Acrobat in Sacramento. I thought I was going to maintain thirty to forty hours, and I would get less. There were even times where I wouldn't work for a week or two. I tried to take advantage of the time and write more. However, not having the money to do what I wanted to do forced me to think I should stay home to conserve money and gas.

I remembered that because of all those things, I found myself increasingly lonely and highly depressed. In such cases, I would close myself off from the world, push friends away, and bury myself in online applications. Sometimes I would find myself hanging out with women who would do nothing for me, but they made me feel better until I didn't want them around anymore.

During that time, I would only eat when I was at work. I had purchased Sacramento Kings tickets, which threw my finances out of sync. I would also have debt collectors call me for student loan payments. To make my money situation worse, my car blew a head gasket and I had to get another car. I was able to purchase a Ford Explorer from my cousin for $150. However, I was spending $60 every three or four days just to drive from Oak Park to Rocklin. It forced me to quit my job in Rocklin after ten months working there and return to Acrobat, which at the time had better hours.

Regardless of these issues, I always forced myself to step back and look at myself through another person's eyes. Sometimes that was the only way I could see the good things I'd actually done in the community and for myself.

I never was without a car. I stayed employed at all times, whether it was with Acrobat or with other jobs. I always had a place, on my own or with my parents.

I was also never without some sort of community. Before going to prison camp, I became active in my Prince Hall Masonic Lodge. Upon my return, I became active again and their fellowship helped me through some hard times.

I joined a group called Greater Sacramento Urban League Young Professionals, a group of young Black professionals who were active in politics, community service, and supporting businesses in the Sacramento area.

I was also mildly active in the poetry and artists community in Sacramento. I couldn't attend all their functions, but I would give donations to as many of their causes as possible while improving my open mic and poetry skills. I also attended several events and slowly built relationships with the artists and entrepreneurs in the area.

Though I'm not Christian, I would also volunteer at my Masonic brothers' church, Faith Covenant Community Church. I would help with feeding the homeless or with their fireworks stand or whatever I could do when time permitted.

I also became active in an organization called Sacramento ACT (Area Congregations Together). Sac ACT is a multicultural, multi-faith grassroots organization that empowers everyday people to create a more healthy and just community. ACT has a division called Live Free where they fight against mass incarceration and help felons reestablish themselves in the community.

During those two years, I found myself on an emotional rollercoaster. However, I always did something positive and fruitful. I was a person who never really gave up on my dreams, regardless of the odds against me or my personal frustrations.

When I reported my community service work and proved that I had routinely paid my restitution to my PO, he told me that I could get my five-year supervised release reduced to two years if I found a steady job. A month later, I was hired at the Valley Hi Country Club and at the Old Spaghetti Factory, both as dishwashers.

On July 30, I went to my PO's office, took a final drug test, and gave him my check stubs, which proved my employment. In October 2014, I was released from federal supervised release. I then terminated my employment with those two jobs to focus on working for Acrobat in Sacramento and in the Bay Area. In August 2015, I was hired as a busser at a high-end restaurant called Land Ocean in Roseville, California. The commute was about 45 to 90 minutes; however, it was a great-paying job. I also focused on my career as a writer as well as other community service activities.

About the Author

Pyerse Dandridge was born in Sacramento, California. He received his bachelor's degree in English from Sacramento State University. He currently blogs at his website pyersedandridge.com and volunteers his time to Sacramento ACT.

Made in the USA
Middletown, DE
16 January 2019